The Oblivious Obvious

By
J. M. Friedli

2016

My sincere thanks go to
my brothers for their honesty,
my parents for their support & guidance,
my friends for their companionship,
and to my loved one for all of the above.

Contents

OPENING WORDS — 1
- Why am I writing this? — 1
- Where did I get the information? — 3
- Where will the money go? — 4
- What are the future plans? — 4

CHAPTER 1: THE EQUATION OF THOUGHTFULNESS — 5
- Intro — 6
- Acceptance — 7
- Hope — 9
- Progress — 11
- Value Of This Framework — 13

CHAPTER 2: EVERYTHING YOU DO — 14
- Intro — 15
- TER-Pyramid — 16
- Trade-Offs — 26
- Closing Thoughts — 42

CHAPTER 3: KNOWING — 43
- Intro — 44
- Direct and Indirect Sources — 46
- Knowledge Acquisition Treatment — 46
- Impact of the Unknown — 48
- Knowledge Processing — 51
- Learning and Contributing — 52
- Closing Thoughts — 54

CHAPTER 4: THINKING — 55
- Intro — 56
- Sphere A — 61

Sphere B	76
Excursion - The Interpretation Benefit	90
Sphere C	93
Excursion - Control within the framework	98
Closing Thoughts	100

CHAPTER 5: PROBLEMS & OUTCOMES — 101

Intro	102
The Meaning of Problems	103
Your Problems	105
Priority of Problems	110
Prioritizing your problems	113
Confronting Problems	115
Impact of the Path Not Taken	118
Closing Thoughts	121

CHAPTER 6: THE ESSENTIAL EIGHT — 122

Intro	123
Self-Control	124
Humility	128
Tolerance	130
Feedback	133
Time	138
Change	141
Love	145
Freedom	148

CHAPTER 7: GUIDANCE FOR A MEANINGFUL LIFE — 150

Personal Interpretation of the	151
Meaning of Life	151

LAST THOUGHTS — 157

Opening Words

Why am I writing this?

I was hoping that life would become less clouded and more manageable. Not before long, I came to realize that we may be living in an era with the least amount of complexity seen so far.

Approximately thirty years from now, my children might be the same age as I am today. They will grow up in a world that has become more interconnected and advanced, yet also more perplexing. My children, along with the rest of the world, will be driven by the sophisticated and the mind-bending, overwhelmed by information and complexity, and blind to the obvious. Namely, the fundamental ways of thinking that everything is based upon.

I want to help. As early as I can.

The purpose of this book is to offer simple insights about thoughtfulness and guidance that remain true during increasingly dynamic times. Since my children have not yet been born, this book is thirty years before its time. Consequently, I started to focus on the simple & certain as opposed to the complicated & unsure. In other words, I sacrificed specificity for generality to obtain meaningful insights that are always applicable to everyone - and thus, continue to be relevant for my children in thirty years.

Fundamentals are the greatest gift in a time of complexity.

Where did I get the information?

Two years ago, I started to take notes on various insights that were shared with me hoping I could someday pass them on. My goal became to extract the universally true & always applicable from the clutter. This forced me to discard most of the knowledge that I previously recorded. It simply might not have been able to stand the test of time.

I never intended to explore the potentially rewarding uncertainty to inspire progress; I wanted to refocus on the constants in the hope it might help as well.

External works do not underlie the same purpose, and consequently, were of limited use to me. So, I decided not to use external sources.

I simply sat at a table for days on end, asking myself what will always hold true about the actions, the thinking and the decisions that I have encountered thus far in my life, that will be relevant for my children.

The question was: "What will hold true for the next 30 years that is worth knowing then?"

Part of the answer is this book.

Where will the money go?

All the income that I will generate from the sale of this book, whether in paper form or online, will directly go to the Three F Foundation, a charitable organization that aims to provide access to education for youths around the world.

What are the future plans?

While I have invested a lot of time and exerted the upmost effort into writing this book, it will not be without flaws. In its attempt to incorporate concepts that are both always true and meaningful, it will not be perfect or complete.

I wholeheartedly welcome any feedback about this book. You can submit your thoughts about new concepts or adjustments to the current ones vie email at: www.theobliviousobvious@gmail.com

In my commitment to provide my offspring with the most relevant and most valuable content, I envision updated versions of this book to be published in five-year intervals. These updated versions will include the valuable feedback I will receive in the next five years, accredited accordingly, as well as other new insights worth passing on.

Chapter 1: The Equation of Thoughtfulness

Intro

The single most impactful insight that I have been fortunate enough to gain is illustrated below.

$$\frac{(T + 1) * K}{T} = \left(\frac{\infty}{1}\right)$$
$$T=1$$
$$K<1$$

The formula is a combination of three simple and important insights that are the foundation for thoughtfulness.

I converted these concepts into mathematical terms and was thus able to derive a rather simple equation, considering the extent of information that lies beneath the numbers.

These individual insights, as well as the overarching mathematical equation, are true in every situation and at any point in time, throughout one's life.

Now, what does it all mean?

Acceptance

Every single occurrence that has happened up to this point in time cannot be altered in any way and will persist.

Thus, there is no use in trying to change or thinking about changing what has happened. It is outside of your control, outside the realm of possible, and definitely not worth your time - and neither is denying or discarding what has happened.

The only thing to do for anyone at any point in time is to unconditionally accept that what has happened right up until that particular point in time is unchangeable. This understanding, which is obvious to some, directly guides your reaction to the world around you.

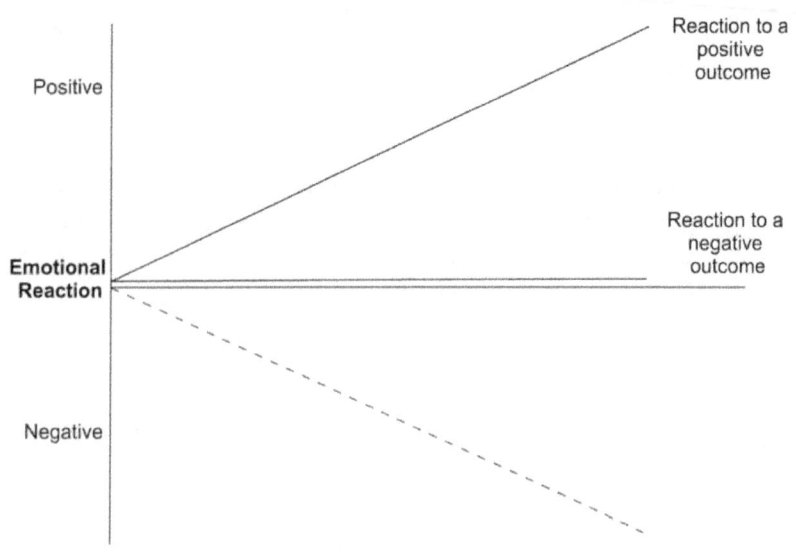

Ideal Approach
If a positive event occurred, you may rejoice depending on how positive the event was. Conversely, if it is negative, there is no inherent need for a negative emotional reaction, as it will simply not impact what has happened. In other words, it will not influence the past (i.e. T-1).

Conclusion
Any attempt to change what has happened, any thought about changing, as well as the negative emotional reaction aimed at the past, make no inherent sense.

The denominators on both sides of the equation illustrate this first insight. T is 1. Meaning, what has happened up to point T in time has only one outcome.

$$\frac{(T+1) * K}{T} = \left(\frac{\infty}{1}\right)$$

$T=1$
$K<1$

⬅ Acceptance

In summary so far: **It is how it is.**

Keep in mind that translating this insight into action requires little active focus, as it is more of an attitude. Further, acceptance does not mean you should not learn from the past, in fact, accepting what has happened encourages you to do so.

Hope

At any moment in time you have unlimited options moving forward.

In knowing that the past cannot be altered: you are now faced with the possible ways to respond to what has happened. The options to move forward always come from the following sources:

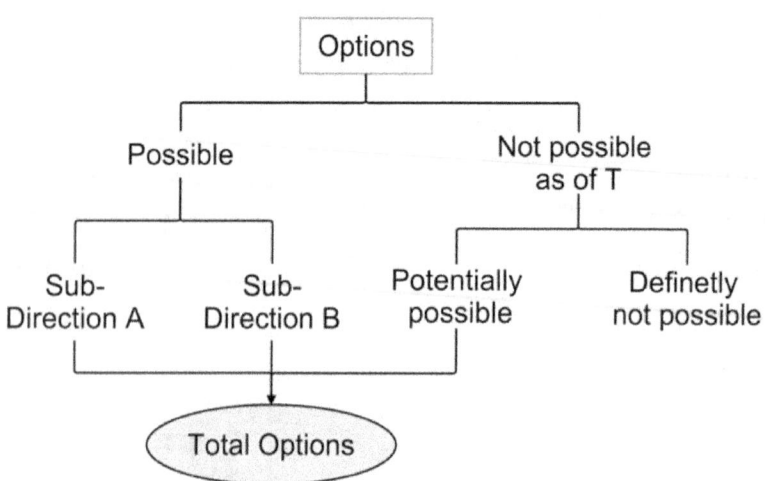

Ideal Approach
Ideally, you will first separate the possible from the impossible options as of right now (Time = T). Then, it makes sense to understand the general directions of the sub options. In other words, in what general way could my decision go: sub-direction A or B? There is also a second source of options, those that have not become possible yet, but might become possible in T+1.

Conclusion

This insight is about knowing that, at any point, there are many, if not infinite options moving forward that are within your control. These options consist of what is possible now and what might be possible in the future. It is not about eliminating options.

$$\frac{(T+1) * K}{T} = \left(\frac{\infty}{1}\right)$$

← Hope

$T=1$
$K<1$

The numerators of the equation illustrate this; T+1 is infinite. It illustrates that the possibilities of moving forward are endless. In other words, T+1 has infinite outcomes.

In Summary so far: **It is how it is, and many options exist.**

Keep in mind that translating this insight into action requires active focus, experience, common sense and wisdom. Finding options in T and in T+1 are essentially a prerequisite for the next, rather obvious step.

Progress

All but one of the options is inferior to all other options.

Naturally, the next step is to find an option that will dictate your behaviour. Of all the possible options, there is one that inevitably stands out. It is an action whose consequences best align with the motives established by you, and that will bring you as close as possible to a desired outcome. In other words, it is the best option moving forward. How can that one option be identified?

Ideal Approach
Identifying the right option is the key to everything. Unfortunately, nobody will be able to provide a definite revelation in that regard. Nonetheless, the appeal of thoughtfulness and the drive to consciousness in the pages that follow should provide guidance on how to move forward.

$$\underset{\substack{T=1 \\ K<1}}{\frac{(T+1)*K}{T} = \left(\frac{\infty}{1}\right)}$$

(Progress ↓)

The constant K that reduces the amount of possibilities in T+1 illustrates this. In other words, not all paths are worth pursuing.

In summary: **It is how it is, many options exist, and few paths arise.**

Keep in mind that this is where most of the focus should be.

Value Of This Framework

Even though the framework only introduces a general overview, I have found these concepts to be meaningful, as they are applicable in every situation at any time with no exceptions.

This equation of thoughtfulness can be something to hold on to, and something that promotes thoughtfulness and consciousness. It advocates clarity which can help you "catch yourself" when life is a bit tough.

Progress ↓

$$\frac{(T+1) * K}{T} = \left(\frac{\infty}{1}\right)$$

⬅ Hope
⬅ Acceptance

$T=1$
$K<1$

In conclusion

It promotes **acceptance**, by realizing that what has happened is unchangeable and
it promotes **hope**, by understanding that the options moving forward are endless and in your control and
it promotes **progress**, by outlining that there must be a path that is superior to the others.

Chapter 2:
Everything you do

Intro

In the chapters to follow, there will be an emphasis on the third insight of the equation of thoughtfulness.

I will never be able to tell you what to think or how you are supposed to think. Nonetheless, I can outline a series of general concepts that fundamentally underlie the thinking that we all do.

Hopefully knowing and understanding these concepts can guide your thinking. Naturally, this is dependent on your personal choice and judgement.

In this chapter, I intend to focus on two concepts that are especially critical, as they will support larger ideas within this book.

TER-Pyramid

The relation of **t**ime, **e**ffort and **r**esult is one of the fundamentals that will be used throughout this book. It judges a decision based on the time spent, the effort made and the result achieved, thereby analysing the worthiness of actions in the past, present and future to achieve deliberate goals.

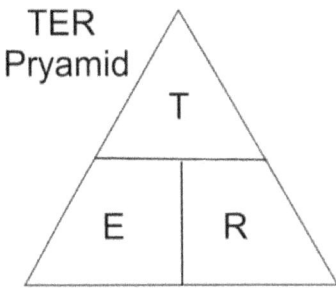

In order to apply the above framework to a variety of situations, the criteria are vague on purpose. Nonetheless, I have attempted to specify these criteria as clearly as possible.

Time
The time spent to obtain a desired result. Time cannot be treated equally among different people. Depending on other activities in one's life, time might become more or less valuable and is thus highly subjective.

Effort
The effort made, the skills needed, the work put in to achieve an outcome. This also includes all the side effects that come along with making the effort.

Result
The reason effort and time was needed. The result can either be a deliberate goal or an unexpected outcome. Further, this also takes into account what you were not able to do within the time needed to achieve the result.

Assessing time, effort and result must be done holistically and is subjective. Every person evaluates 'effort made' differently, interprets 'results achieved' differently and even experiences and values time differently. Thus, it is vital to be cautious when applying this concept to other people than yourself.

All the criteria are essential in deciding whether a decision made sense in the past and whether an action makes sense moving forward.

Interestingly enough, deliberately neglecting one of these criteria will allow us to derive three basic insights that will always be true for all of us. They are worth realizing despite how simple they may seem.

Ignoring Time

We all know that any effort will lead to a result. Ignoring time in deciding if an action makes sense will inhibit you to conclude what result is worth your time. **Remember that not all positive results are worth your time.**

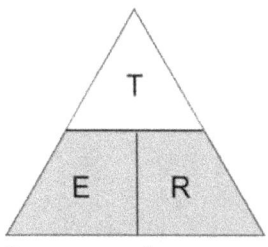

Ignoring Effort

We all know that time is needed to achieve a result. Ignoring effort in deciding if an action is sensible will make you unable to comprehend if the needed effort is worth the result. **Remember that not every positive result is worth putting effort into.**

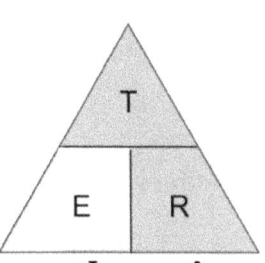

Ignoring Result

We all know that effort simultaneously requires time. Ignoring the result in deciding if an action makes sense will prevent you from determining the effect of the effort exerted and time spent. **Remember that time and effort are not automatically accompanied by a positive result.**

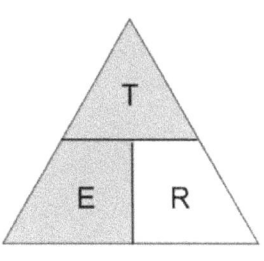

There must be an acceptable balance between these three criteria in order for the action to be worth undertaking. A framework can graphically illustrate this balance.

Using the framework

The question is, how does one assess a correct balance between time, effort and result?

Start with what is most measurable and predictable; Time.

While both effort and result are man-made, time is the only criterion that is outside of your control. In other words, time will be 'spent' regardless of 'effort made' and 'result achieved'.

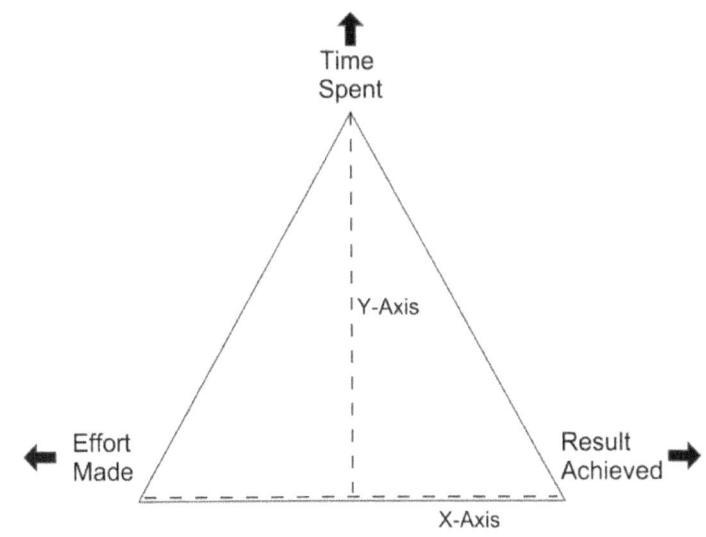

That unique attribute about time has led me to put it on top of the pyramid. Now, imagine time spent as being measured on the y-axis, effort made and result achieved on the x-axis. If you envision the pyramid in that manner, you will be able to assign coordinates to every possible action.

X-Axis: If the result achieved is equal to effort made (regardless of time spent), the coordinate will be on the y-axis (x=0). The more the result achieved outweighs the effort made, the higher is the x-value of the coordinate.

Y-Axis: The more time is needed, the higher the y-value. This depends on the time scope that will be discussed shortly.

Assigning the coordinates will reveal the action's worthiness.

Theoretically, the point (0,0) along with any point on the x-axis cannot exist, because every action requires at least some time. For the sake of usefulness, we will assume that when time is equal to zero (y=0), almost no time was spent.

As illustrated below, there is an area within the triangle where all the coordinates automatically deem the corresponding action as worthy.

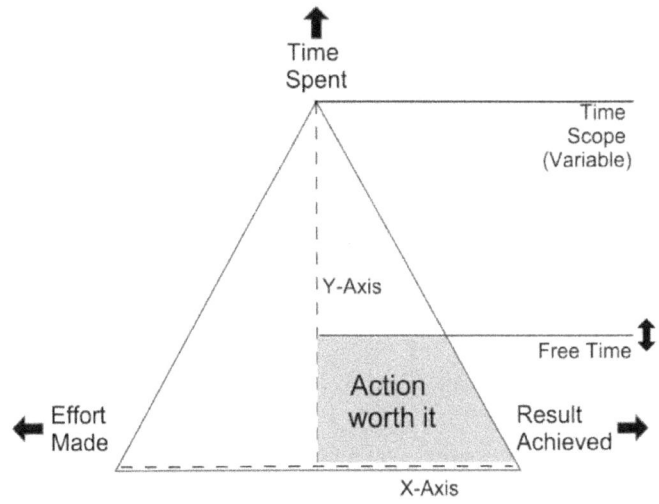

In this area, the result achieved must outweigh the effort made, as you also invested your time and should be compensated for that. Thus, the area will always be to the right of the y-axis and above the x-axis. The missing limitation to the area is time, which fortunately for us, is the criterion that is most easily measured and predicted.

The final step is to assign a time scope to your graphical interpretation of an action's worthiness.

Time Frame

The idea here is to establish a time frame within which you can evaluate a decision. While you can adjust the time scope, a 12-hour time scope is a good starting point.

Free Time Constraint

The last aspect is the free time constraint. Within your time scope, you will only have a certain amount of disposable time in which you can control what actions to undertake. Naturally, the less time that you have at your disposal, the smaller the area becomes.
You are left with a graphical representation of an area, in which all coordinates will deem the corresponding action as worthy.

Correctly assessing the Y-value

It is the most time you would spend for the desired result given the external parameter (in our case 12 hours). Ask yourself, what is the most time you are prepared to invest for the result, in relation to your time scope.

If the answer is within the free time constraint, and possible during that time, the action should be undertaken.

Decision

When faced with a possible action ensure that the result achieved outweighs the effort made (1). Then, focus on the time that is at your disposal and that is within your control (2). Ask yourself, what is the maximum time that you would spend for achieving the result given the parameter that you have set yourself? (3). Only then think about the time requirement of the action itself (4).

If it is within the fourth area, undertaking the action will be worth it.

If multiple actions make sense simultaneously, it is a question of prioritization, which will be covered extensively in Chapter 5.

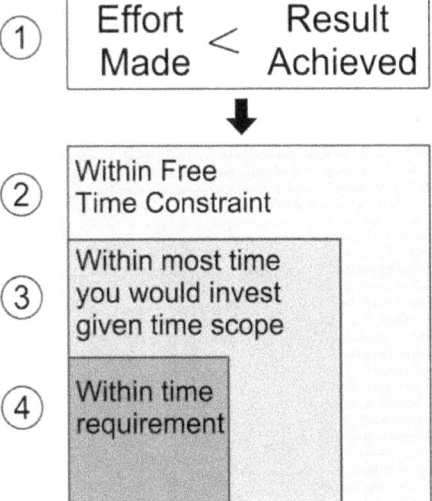

Another Useful Angle

Remember that effort over time must be equal to reward over time. In other words, the benefit over time unit must be equal or greater than the effort per time unit for the action to be worthwhile.

$$\frac{\text{Effort}}{\text{Time}} \leq \frac{\text{Result}}{\text{Time}}$$

Trade-Offs

The outcome of every action can either be digital (yes or no) or it can be qualitative, meaning there are different degrees of fulfilment.

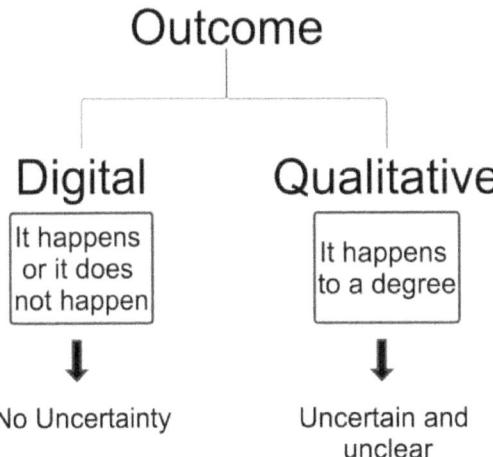

In reality, qualitative outcomes and digital outcomes are closely interrelated.

Digital to Qualitative
Taking an action with a qualitative outcome is in itself a digital action. In other words, you have taken the action or you have not taken the action.

Qualitative to Digital
A qualitative result can include a series of digital outcomes. In other words, within the degree of fulfilment, there are certain aspects that were achieved and others that were not achieved.

This distinction will not only lead to more clarity and a better understanding of the outcomes in your life, but will also depict where the real challenge lies.

If all actions had digital results, the outcomes of your actions could be more easily steered to what you want them to be. In other words, you would have more control over the result of your actions. There would be less uncertainty.

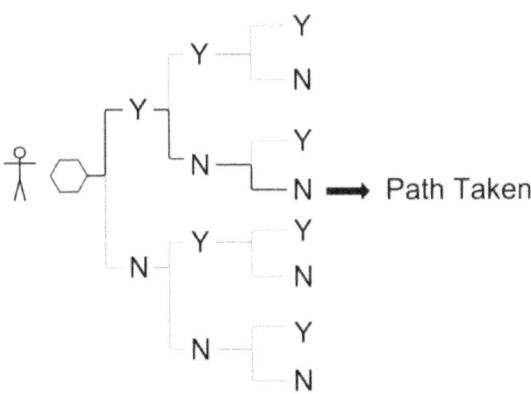

If all the results were qualitative, the outcome of your action would be a more difficult one to know in advance. It might not be what you want it to be. In other words, you would have to make more room for uncertainty and accept some loss of control.

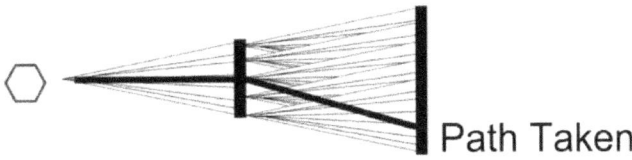

As we all know, our actions have both digital and qualitative results. The crucial part is to realize that when it comes to decision-making, you will either be faced with a qualitative or a digital outcome. In other words, you will have at most three choices.

As illustrated below, when an action results in a digital outcome you can either decide to have the outcome occur or decide not to have it occur. Conversely, actions that will lead to a qualitative result will force you, inevitably, to compromise and undertake a trade-off.

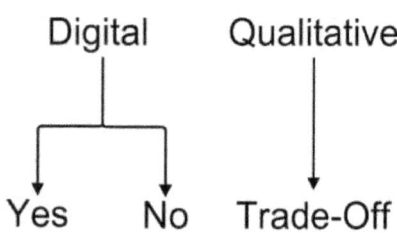

The ability to recognize trade-offs, identify extremes, balance them, and choose a path, is one of the single most relevant skills.

The process of deducing the one path is illustrated below. It often happens subconsciously. Nonetheless, I believe that thoughtfulness entails the need to understand subconscious processes and actively follow them, if appropriate.

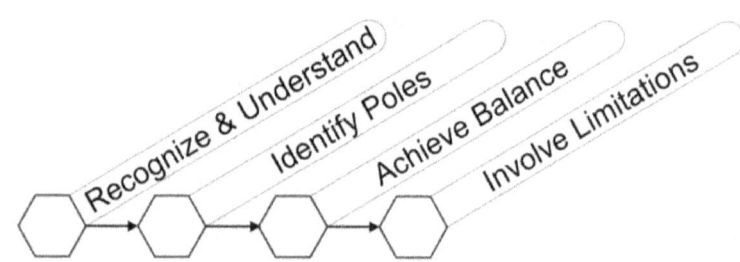

1. Recognizing and Understanding Trade-Offs

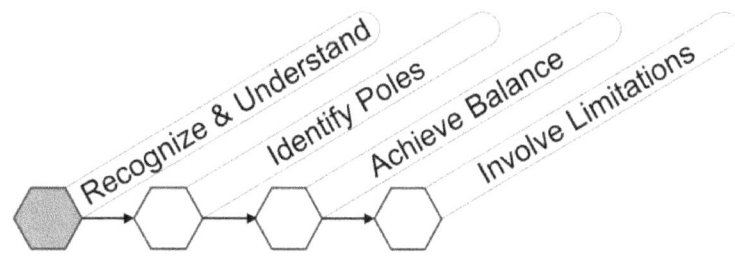

As previously discussed, any action resulting in a qualitative outcome must entail a trade-off. In essence, most of our actions must be, in some way, a balance between two or more opposing poles. The action will always be within that range.

Compromises are inherent in making trade-offs, because you simply cannot have it all. The degree to which you compromise is the differentiating factor.

The decision on how much to compromise is both immensely complicated and deeply personal - and I am far too unwise to write about it.

Nonetheless, there are thousands of trade-offs around us and all of them demand a degree of compromise. Simply knowing that they are there and being cognizant of what exactly you are compromising is of great value.

The real question in addressing a trade-off is what you are really choosing between and how much you want to compromise to achieve a result.

Note

Naturally, you will encounter a series of trade-offs within this book. In order to illustrate how many trade-offs are around us and how different they are in their appearance, I have included the following illustration next to some crucial trade-offs that often underlie or conclude concepts.

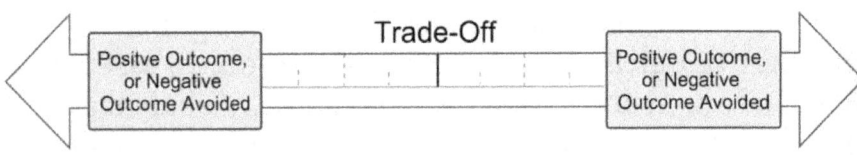

2. The Poles

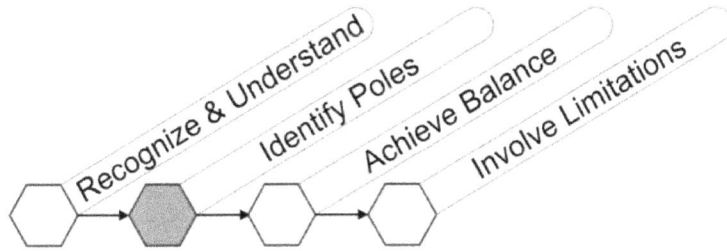

Identifying opposing poles is critical in compromising between them. They must be the most extreme possible paths that relate to the action.

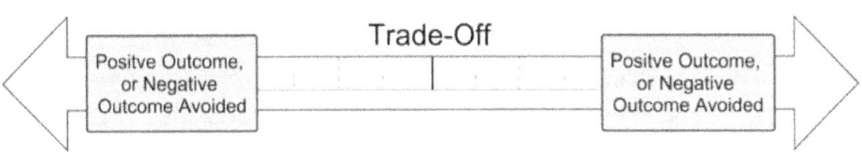

In a trade-off, a pole can be:
a positive outcome that does not avoid anything negative, or
a positive outcome because it avoids something negative.

3. Achieving a Balance

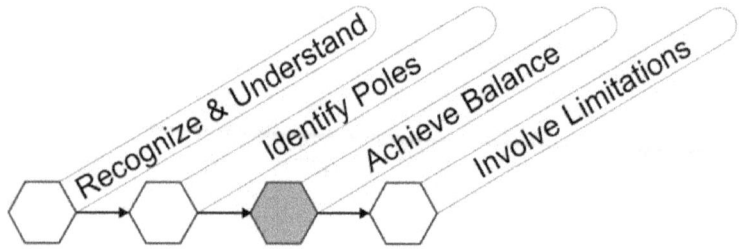

Achieving a balance between the two poles is, as previously mentioned, strongly dependent on one's personal situation, preference and risk tolerance.

Nonetheless, I intend to offer some guidance by making the process of compromising less clouded. Specifically, I will introduce graphical representations of what the trade-offs could look like in hopes that this will enhance clarity and heighten the quality of your decisions.

Achieving a Balance with two Poles

If you are fortunate, you will only need to decide between two opposing poles. In this case, the trade-off will graphically be rather simple.

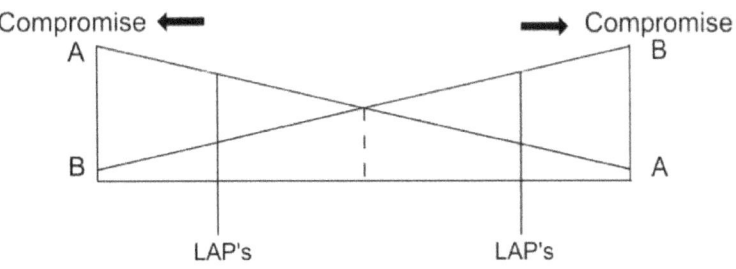

As illustrated above, the two opposing poles are on different sides. As the positive aspect of one diminishes, the other positive aspect will increase.

A useful tool is to imagine the **l**owest **a**cceptable **p**oints (LAP's) for both extremes. This will decrease the parameter within which you must find the optimal path.

In deciding how much to compromise, begin at one of the LAP's and start to gradually move towards the other LAP. Constantly ask yourself if you received more benefit from this compromise or less. As long as the answer is 'yes' continue to compromise, if the answer is 'no' you have reached the optimal point.

It is critical to keep in mind that a compromise is essentially finding a balance between two opposing positive poles.

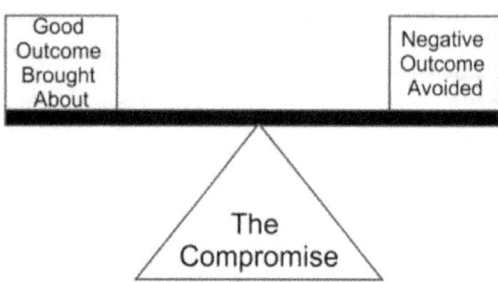

Recognize that there will often be an area between the opposing poles, where you will be unsure if the compromise has an effect, and if so, what that effect is. Within that unknown, you can orient yourself at the two nearest and understood points, but more often than not you must simply let your gut and common sense decide.

Achieving a Balance with three Poles

Naturally, with three poles the issue becomes significantly more complicated and interesting.

As illustrated below, the graphical representation of a trade-off with three opposing poles will be a triangle with equal sides. The extremes are labelled A, B and C.

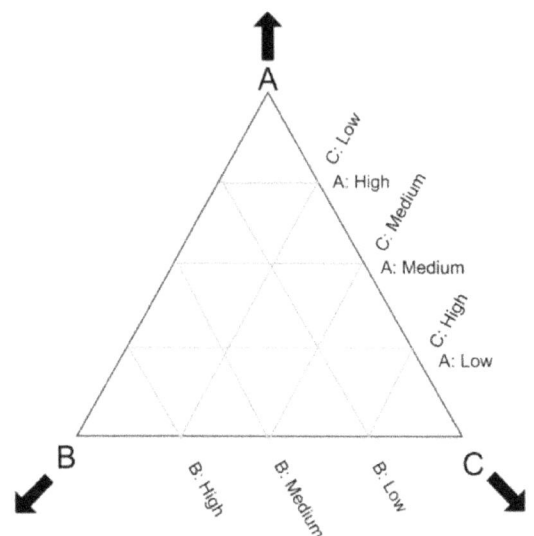

To be able to graphically express where the ideal trade off would be, imagine that the extremes A, B and C are continuously pushing away from each other.

In order to deduce a point within the triangle that represents an adequate trade-off between all three extremes, you have to focus on what you know to be true.

You know how you feel about each extreme individually, and you are thus able to assess their respective importance.

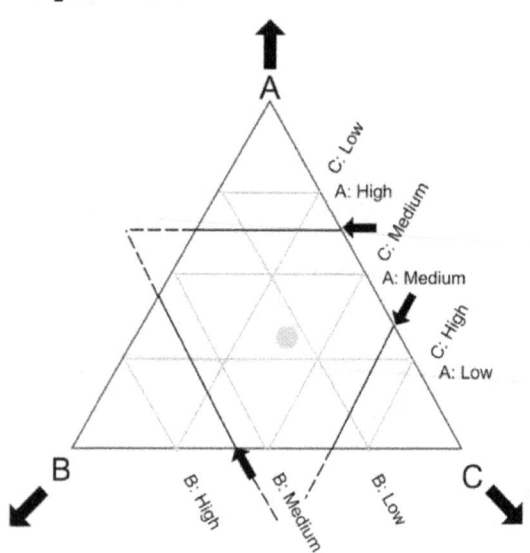

For that purpose, I have included three guidelines that go in each of the three directions. The closer the line is to the pole, the more important the positive extreme is to you.

After reviewing each extreme holistically, you can select a line for every pole, depending on its importance. Interestingly enough, you will begin to see an inverted triangle. Your desired balance will be in the middle of this newly emerged inverted triangle.

4: Involve Time and Digital Limitations

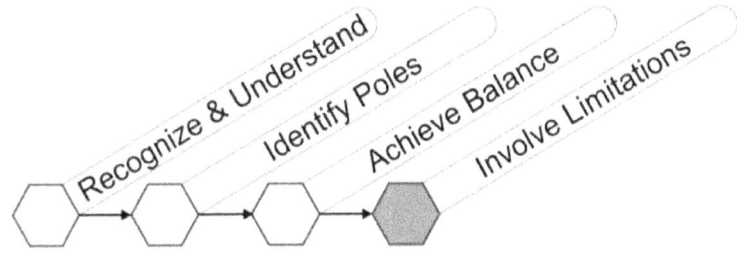

Unfortunately, compromising between two or more options is not as simple as previously illustrated. Two vital concepts complement the process and lead to a more extensive understanding.

Time

The balance of the trade-off should not be solely based upon the poles as of now. There must be some focus on how both poles will be impacted throughout time. For whatever reason, the poles might become more or less extreme.

Fact is, the chosen compromise to achieve the current balance, might not be the compromise that leads to the same balance in the future. Ideally, this would be taken into account at T to achieve the right balance at T+1.

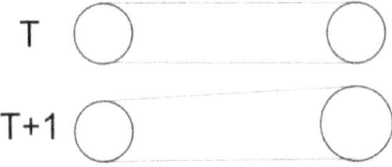

The better you can capture the movements of the poles, the more accurate the compromise and the decision will be for you.

Granted, it is very difficult to predict the individual poles shifting over time. Nonetheless, knowing that you must take into account those changes is valuable.

Digital Limitations

As previously mentioned, there can be digital outcomes included in more general qualitative outcomes. The possible actions that lie within the parameter of the two poles are neither continuous nor endless. Therefore, you will not always be able to undertake the optimal compromise, as it might not be an option.

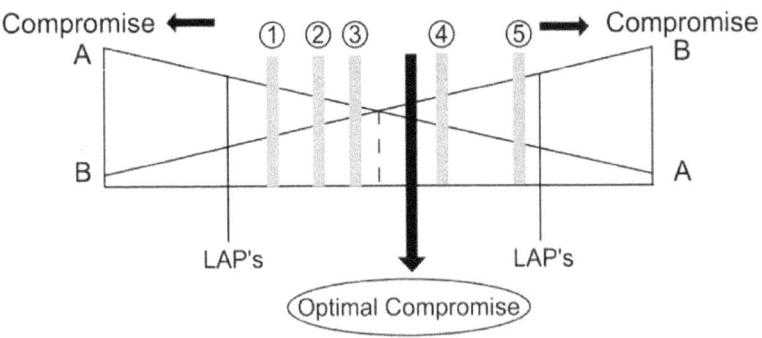

As illustrated above, there are limited options available. There will never be an option that directly corresponds with the optimal path. You will have to settle with the option that is nearest to the optimal point.

This has the following impacts:

You will not be able to compromise exactly how you want, even if you have given it a lot of thought.

You will most likely not be completely content with the trade-off that you have made.

You might be wondering, why you did not just simply evaluate the options and their respective compromises and then choose the path that corresponds best with your personal thinking.

The answer is twofold.

Firstly, thinking about the trade-off without including options, will give you a more accurate evaluation of your desired compromise. Focusing on options prematurely tends to distract you from the overall decision you are making; which is between two poles, and not between two options.

Secondly, knowing exactly what compromise you intend to make will equip you with the knowledge of how to adjust the options, if possible. In other words, you cannot only identify the best option, but you will also know in what direction that path falls short of the optimal path. This insight will allow you, if possible, to correct the option in the right direction to more accurately represent your desired compromise.

Closing Thoughts

The relationship between time spent, effort made and result achieved can determine the worthiness of actions in the past, present and future. The aforementioned framework will allow you to graphically infer which actions make sense for you, given your free time constraint and your subjective interpretation of effort and result.

Recognizing the trade-offs, as well as the opposing poles, is a great step towards thinking thoughtfully and making sensible decisions. Over time, you will develop the common sense required to fully leverage those concepts through actions you have undertaken and lessons you have learned along the way.

The provided graphical frameworks, along with the understanding of how your desired compromise is interconnected with time and the availability of options, will hopefully give your dealing with trade-offs more clarity.

Chapter 3: Knowing

Intro

At any point in time, we have a certain amount of knowledge. It affects absolutely everything we do. Nonetheless, we have a habit not to think about what we know, its quality, or its impact.

Understanding your own knowledge, along with its strengths and limitations, will enable you to think more clearly. This clarity is another essential step towards thoughtfulness.

All the knowledge you have ever obtained, everything you have ever learned, can only come from a small number of sources, as illustrated below.

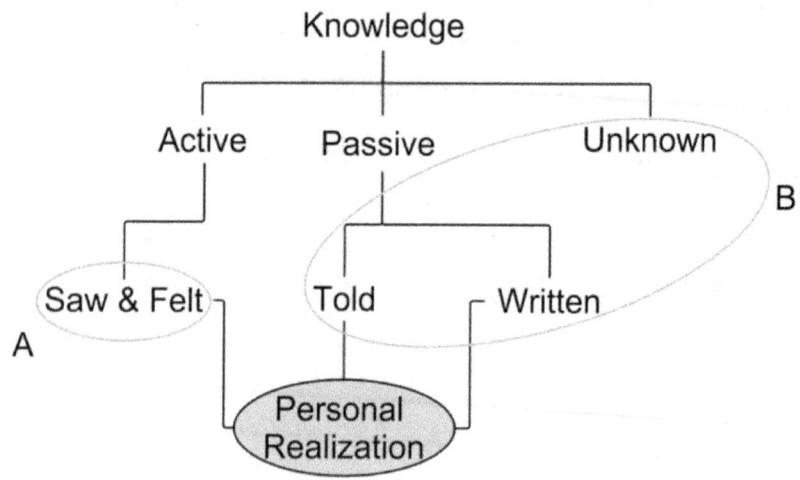

There are a number of conclusions that we can draw based on this graph.

Direct and Indirect Sources

When you see something, you know what you saw. When you feel something, physically or emotionally, you know how it felt. Specifically, with active knowledge you are directly at its source. In other words, you can validate the accuracy of the information yourself.

On the other hand, with passive knowledge you are either told something, or you read something that transfers into personal knowledge. Even though you retain information, you did not have any direct contact to the source of knowledge. In other words, you cannot validate the correctness of the information yourself right away.

Knowledge Acquisition Treatment

These different origins of information, will lead to distinct treatments of the knowledge. Since direct information is already validated by yourself, the next step is to interpret.

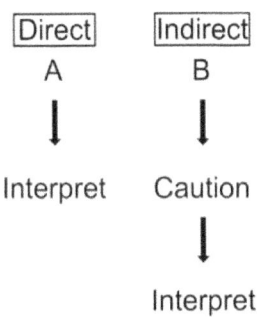

However, with indirect information there is no validation of its accuracy and you cannot simply interpret. Instead, you need to acquire the information with caution, remember that it is not validated, critically review it if necessary, and only then interpret.

Impact of the Unknown

It is often forgotten that knowledge also consists of what you do not know. Regardless of whether you know something or not, it might impact an outcome that is relevant to you.

Naturally, it is impossible for people to know what they do not know. Nonetheless, it should impact your attitude before and after you make a statement or a decision.

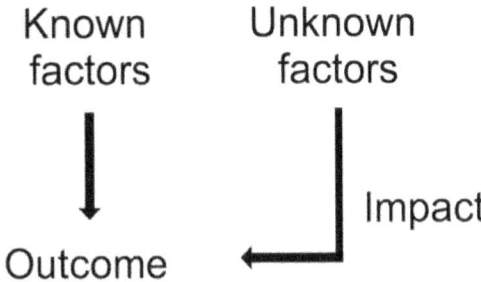

Before the outcome has occurred (at T)

The unknown will inevitably have an impact on the outcome of your actions and decisions, which you will not be able to assess. Even though this impact is outside of your control, it still affects, to a small or great extent, the end result.

After the outcome has occurred (at T+1)

Furthermore, even after the event, when the outcome has occurred, you will only have a partial insight into what has happened.

You might be able to understand the previously unknown factors that influenced the outcome, which is often insightful.

Nonetheless, not all the factors will be apparent as soon as the outcome has happened. You will always be oblivious to the impact of some unknown factors that influenced the outcome, even after the outcome has occurred.

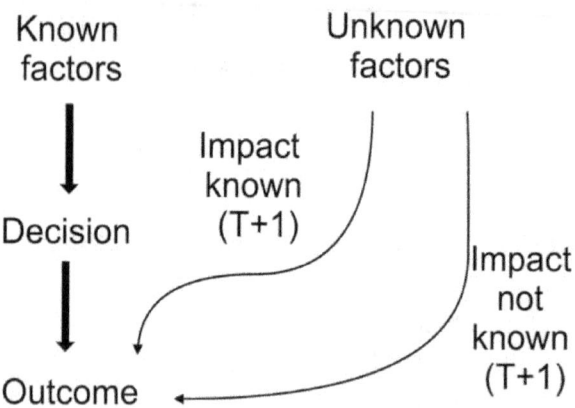

In conclusion, it is not possible to assess the impact of the unknown on the outcome before or even after the outcome has occurred, whether good or bad. This insight suggests that we should be more cautious and more humble before and after every outcome.

This includes: taking less credit when the outcome is good, and blaming yourself less when the outcome is bad.

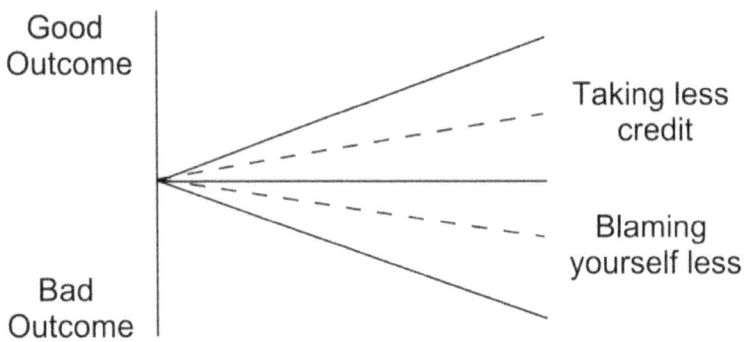

Knowledge Processing

As soon as you have acquired knowledge, you can treat it in several ways. You can either remember it in its unchanged form, or choose to enrich the knowledge. Knowledge enrichment occurs by adjusting the information depending on your personal preferences or by creating completely new knowledge. The choice is yours.

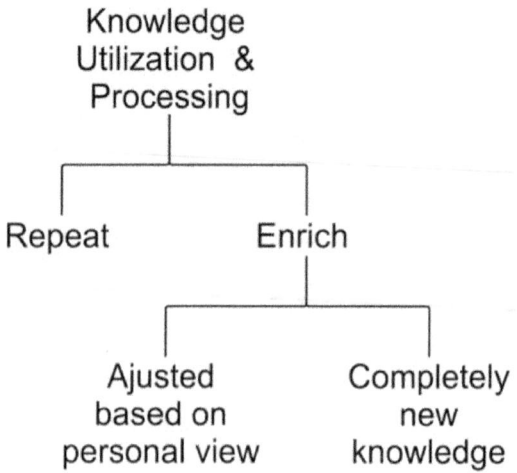

Personal realization often happens unconsciously. It is the result of combining both direct and indirect information. When choosing to enrich the knowledge you have, remember how it was acquired and the corresponding need for caution.

Learning and Contributing

At any point in time, a person is either providing knowledge to others or receiving knowledge from others. During a set time frame, there is a trade-off between learning and contributing, which needs to be balanced.

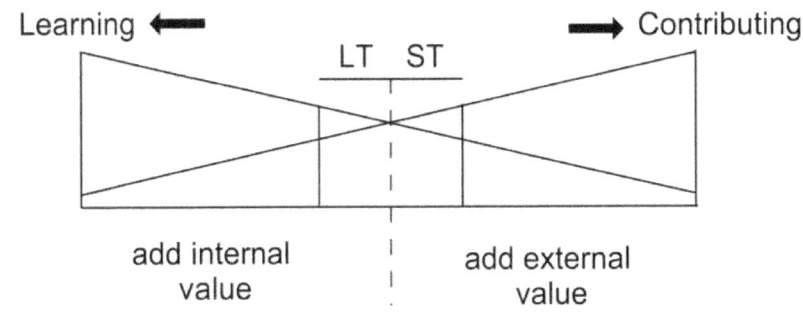

When you are contributing, specifically when you are writing, talking, or demonstrating how something is done, you are not learning in its purest sense. You simply repeat what you already know; you are not obtaining new knowledge.

When you are learning, specifically when you are reading, listening or being shown how something is done, you are not contributing. You are simply absorbing what you do not know; you are creating knowledge for yourself.

Naturally, any knowledge that you have may lead to self-realizations, which can occur before, during or after these two processes.

The question that arises is: where on the scale is the ideal place to be, in order to maximize the total value during a set period of time?

While the left side of the spectrum creates internal value for you, the right side creates external value. A balance near the middle will inevitably create the most value.

The aspect of time should be included in our approach to balancing the trade-off. Since acquiring internal value will more likely add to higher external value in the future, it can be seen as long-term value creation. On the other hand, adding external value will simply contribute in the short-term, which can be just as useful.

Closing Thoughts

The importance of thinking about your knowledge, its quality, and its impact, cannot be overstated.

The focus in this chapter was on the sources of knowledge, its initial treatment depending on those origins, the impact of the unknown, the knowledge processing and lastly the relation between learning and contributing.

The insights about caution and attitude are of paramount importance. Since the aforementioned concepts are always applicable and true, they are worth knowing and may even guide your thinking, if you let them of course.

Chapter 4: Thinking

Intro

There is a tendency to avoid reflecting about how you process information or how you think. The structure of one's thought process is incredibly complex and widely documented. However, the fundamental concepts of thinking have been widely considered obvious, and are oftentimes neglected.

In the following pages, I have outlined the overall thinking process in three spheres, each of which contains a series of insights that may guide your thinking process.

Overview

The process of thinking entails the following: obtaining knowledge, processing it and conveying it, if necessary. An overview and framework that promotes clear thinking is outlined below.

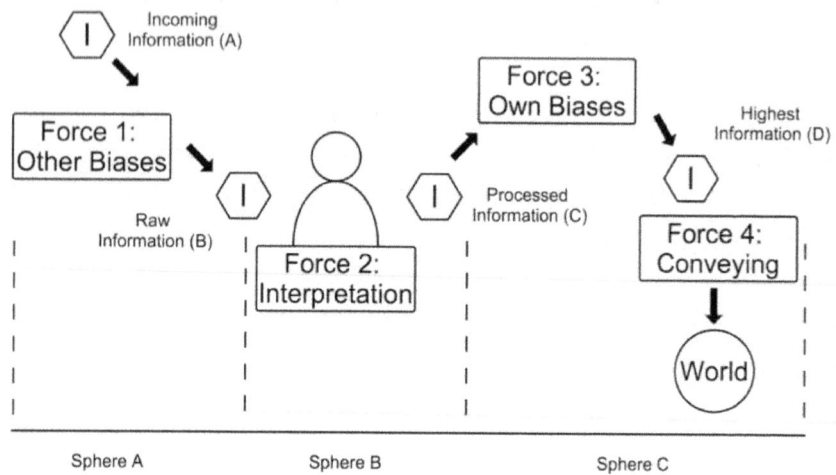

Four Forces

It is critical to realize that any information exchanged that involves human beings is false to a certain degree. As knowledge travels through you to the world, four forces tend to impact the information along the way. This is illustrated above. Each of these forces corrupt the information to a certain extent.

Understanding how these four forces influence the information that you receive and send will bring structure and clarity to your thinking process. Further, it will call attention to critical points within the framework where more caution is necessary.

Quality Information

The quality of the information throughout the thinking process is critical. The base of effective thinking is quality information, as outlined below.

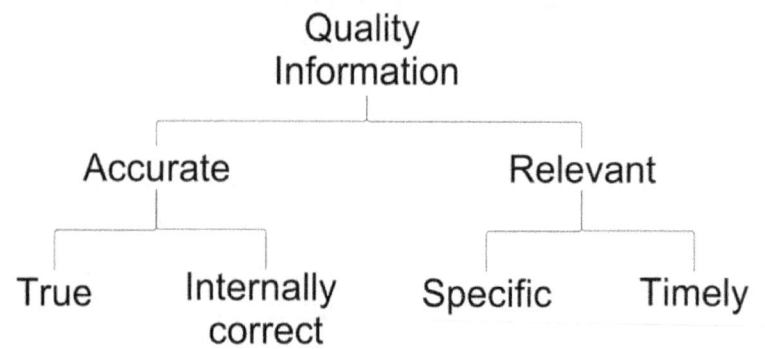

To ensure that the information is accurate, it must be factually true and cannot be subject to biases.

To ensure that the information is relevant, it must create value by targeting the issue and must be significant with respect to time.

In the coming pages, there will be an in-depth discussion of each requirement in its respective sphere.

Guiding Goal

To organize the comprehensive thinking process more clearly, I separated it into three spheres, each with a distinctive guiding goal.

Sphere 1: You clean the incoming information (A) of biases, thereby addressing the requirement of being internally correct.

Sphere 2: You start treating the raw information (B) to ensure it is true, specific and timely. Then you enrich the information in one of the ways outlined. You proceed by ensuring that you are sending quality information to create as much value as possible.

Sphere 3: You clean the processed information (C) of your own biases, thereby addressing the last requirement of being internally correct. Lastly you convey the information (D).

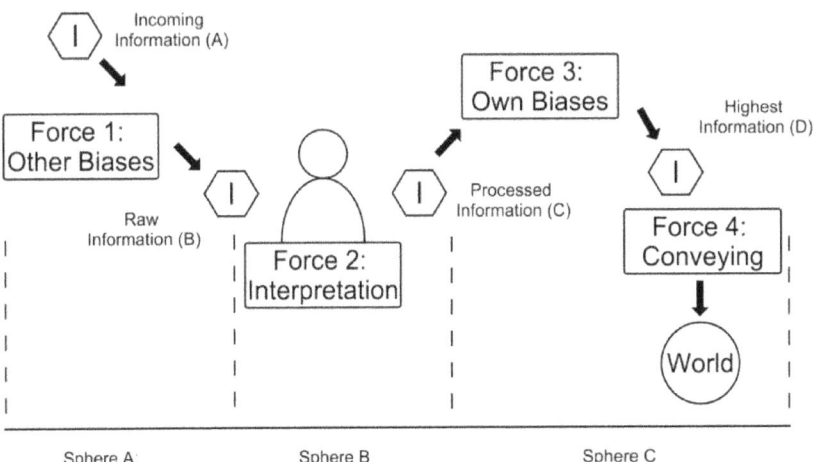

Sphere A

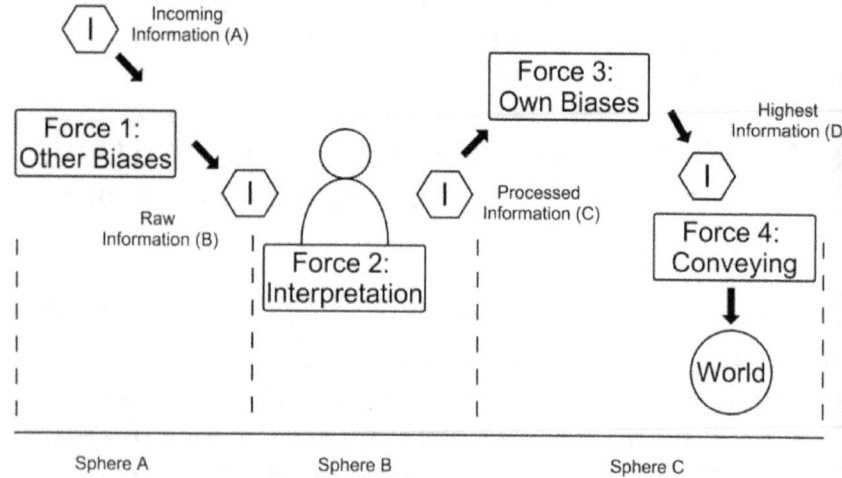

Guiding goal

You clean the incoming information (A) of biases, thereby addressing the requirement of being internally correct. You will obtain raw information (B).

Incoming knowledge can either be quantitative, qualitative or a mix of the two. To simplify things, it can either entail qualitative information or it cannot.

It is crucial to realize that all incoming information is flawed in some way. Some information is simply more or less flawed. For our purposes, it is always of uncertain quality.

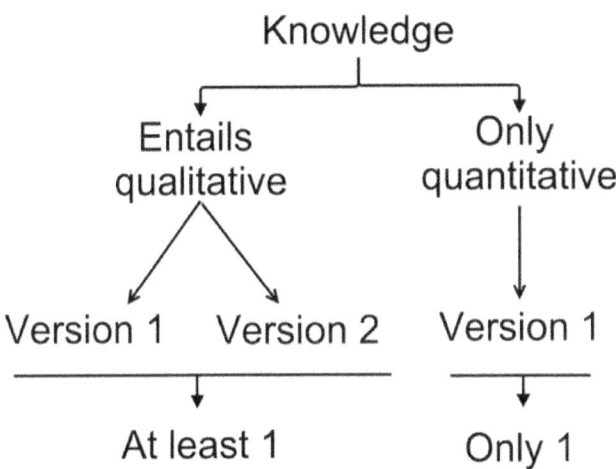

While information that involves qualitative aspects can have multiple versions, quantitative information always has one version. Thus, qualitative information can be more flawed than quantitative information, however, it is not always more flawed.

At this point in the process, quantitative information must be internally correct, as it cannot be contaminated by biases. Unfortunately, qualitative information, whether written or spoken, can be biased. The more complex the qualitative information is, the higher the likelihood of biases. Concepts, ideas or thoughts require personal knowledge, which opens the door for biased thinking.

	Some qualitative	Only quantitative
Internally correct	No	Yes
True	Unsure	Unsure
Specific	Unsure	Unsure
Timely	Unsure	Unsure

Since purely quantitative information does not entail biases, it is automatically raw information (B).

Qualitative information needs to be cleaned of biases in order to be raw information (B). The presence of biases results in the overestimation or underestimation of certain aspects, thereby corrupting the information.

You will need to understand those biases to be able to mitigate their effect on the incoming information. This should be the basis of all your thinking.

Biases

Biases can be categorized as internal or external. The root of the internal biases is directly in the mind. They are caused by the flaws in our own thinking.

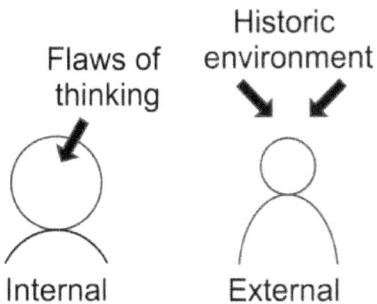

The external biases that impact rational thinking are a result of our environment.

As illustrated below, internal biases can be further subdivided as follows.

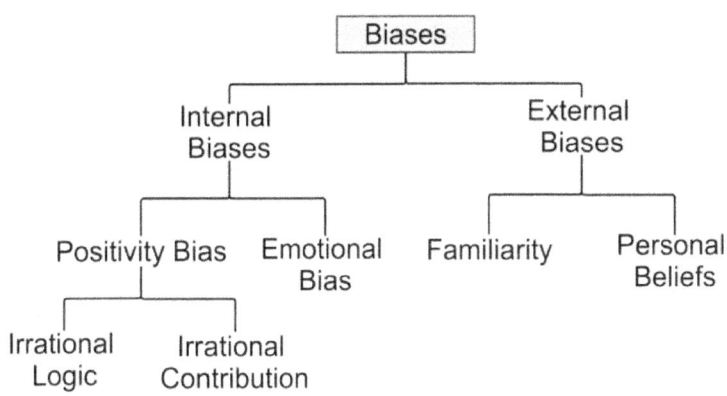

Internal

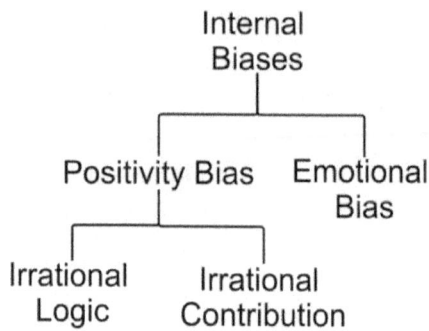

Positivity Bias

There is a tendency to overestimate the positive and underestimate the negative.

In other words, something you want to be impactful - as it would be positive for you - is seen as more impactful than it actually is. Humans are naturally drawn to positivity, and attempt to repel negativity.

The positivity bias can be further subdivided depending on whether a specific outcome is needed for the bias or not.

Irrational Assessment of Contribution

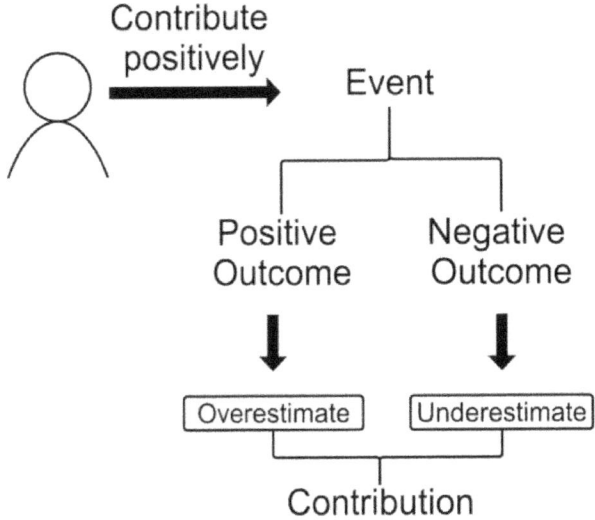

The extent to which people assess the impact of their contribution depends on the outcome of the event. There is a tendency to overestimate the contribution to a positive outcome, and to underestimate the contribution to an event with a negative outcome.

How to correct

Any outcome that is brought about through human effort can create a negative or a positive outcome. Since both the positive and negative result will inevitably lead to irrational thinking, it is wise to imagine the outcome as if it were neither a success nor failure. In this imaginary state, you can assess most clearly what your actual contribution was.

Irrational Assessment of Logic

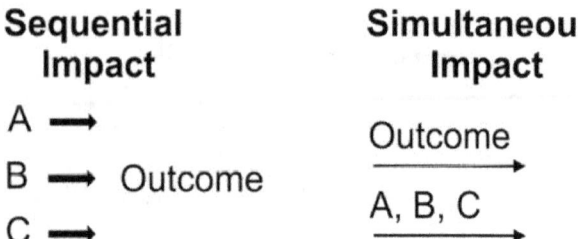

This form of irrational thinking does not depend on the outcome of the event. In other words, it has a permanent impact on us. Further, it is valid for both sequential as well as simultaneous impacts.

If the influence of a logical factor is aligned with your motives, and hence positive in your eyes, it subconsciously becomes overestimated. Similarly, it will be underestimated if it is negative in your eyes.

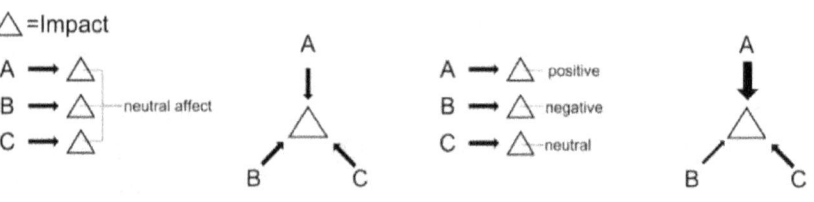

Ideally, the influence of these factors, whether positive or negative to you, is treated proportional to their respective influence.

In reality, you will subconsciously classify the logical factors as positive or negative for your purposes, and overestimate or underestimate their respective influence, as previously illustrated.

How to correct
It is hard, nearly impossible, to eliminate these unconscious effects completely, even if you actively try. Nonetheless, there are two starting points that will help to mitigate their effect to a certain degree.

Simply being cognizant of these subconscious biases will enable you to recognize the more severe impacts of this irrational assessment of logic quite easily.

While these subconscious effects are almost uncontrollable, your individual motive, upon which you compare and identify the factors as positive or negative, is entirely in your control. Ensure that you do not have a strong purpose in mind when you are assessing the impact of a series of logical factors.

Emotional Bias

Naturally, emotions severely motivate biases. Since there are a great variety of different emotions, it is nearly impossible to correctly assess their impact. Nonetheless, I have attempted to provide at least minimal guidance on how to interpret emotions and their corresponding bias.

The Bias of Emotions

	No specific desired outcome	Specific desired outcome
positive	External roots	Interpret according to goal
negative		

We know that emotions make you feel positive or negative towards an issue. Just as important, however, is whether you have a desired outcome in mind or not.

This aspect crucially differentiates these emotional biases. An emotional reaction with a goal in mind can be interpreted according to the desired outcome of the subject, if known. On the other hand, an emotional reaction that does not entail a specific desired outcome always has its roots externally. Thus, it should not be considered and dismissed.

External

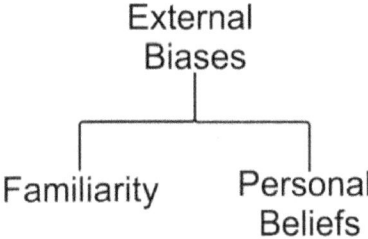

In many ways, the external cultural and economic environment shapes people's thoughts and results in biases.

It directly affects what people know and what they are familiar with, and how knowledge is used to derive qualitative information in the form of personal beliefs.

As illustrated above, the internal factors can be further sub-divided into familiarity and personal beliefs.

Familiarity

We all are naturally drawn to certainty, and scared by uncertainty. People have always had a tendency to prefer options with more information to those with less. In other words, they typically prefer the known to the unknown.

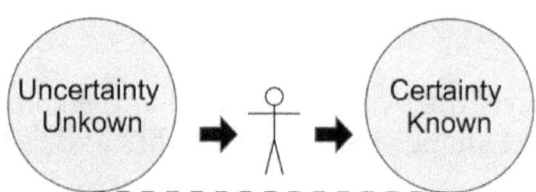

We tend to overestimate the certain and known factors, while simultaneously underestimating the uncertain and unknown factors. That is why the external environment plays such a vital role. The cultural and economic upbringing directly affects what people know, and what they are accustomed to.

How to correct
The economic and cultural environment will always impact what you know. Being familiar to everything, which is not possible, would eliminate this bias. Thus, we must take the other, more difficult path, of assuming nothing and questioning everything.

Attempt to look at the issue as an independent third party that is not familiar to either the known or unknown. Question everything that you know and think to be certain. Treating both the familiar and the unfamiliar equally is the closest you can get to rational thinking.

Personal Beliefs

What you know is a direct result of your environment. Not everything you know is considered to be true by you, and not everything that is considered to be true, is based on actual knowledge. This curious fact is illustrated below.

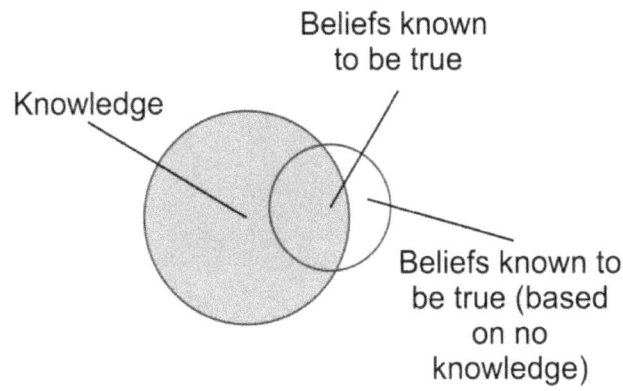

What you believe to be true automatically influences how you process information. Nonetheless, not knowing where beliefs originate and how true they really are, poses a threat to rational thinking.

The beliefs that you consider to be true are derived from two sources.

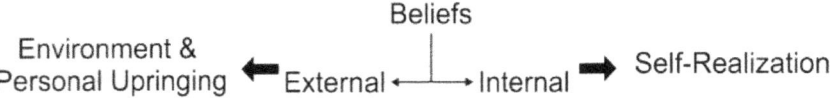

The external beliefs have been passed on to you throughout your personal upbringing and your surrounding environment. The rest of your beliefs are internal. In other words, you realized them on your own or adjusted beliefs, based on information you had.

In either case, you are left with beliefs that you consider to be true.

Logical factors that support what you consider to be true will be internally perceived as positive and thus according to the logical bias, overestimated. Conversely, logical factors that contradict what you consider to be true will be underestimated.

How to correct

It is crucial to understand that what you consider to be true, while highly subjective, guides your thinking. To mitigate the effect of your personal beliefs, it is critical that you are cognizant of their existence and the situations when they impact your thinking excessively.

Further, you need to differentiate between the universally true and the subjectively true. Universal truths serve an important role in rational thinking, whereas the subjectively true is substantially less useful and should only be used with caution.

Unfortunately, the subjectively true is often disguised as universally true. Ideally, you would be able to recognize these situations and react accordingly. In other words, identify subjectively true knowledge by retaining that "it is believed to be A," not, "It is A."

Summary

As you may recall, our goal was to clean incoming information (A) of biases, thereby addressing the requirement of it to be internally correct. As of now, our information is as follows.

	Some qualitative	Only quantitative
➤ Internally correct	No	Yes
True	Unsure	Unsure
Specific	Unsure	Unsure
Timely	Unsure	Unsure

By understanding these internal and external biases, and by knowing how to correct them, it is possible to obtain information that is internally correct.

This information is the first step to our overall goal of thinking clearly in a world full of noise. Further, it serves as the ideal starting point for Sphere B in our overall framework.

Sphere B

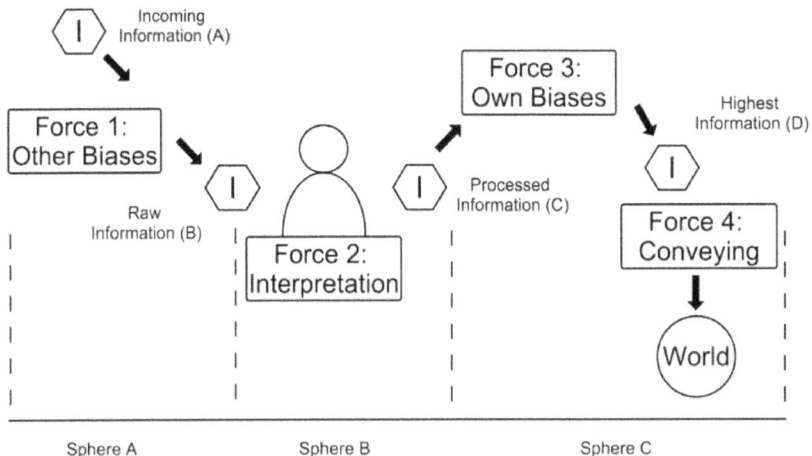

Guiding goal

You start treating the raw information (B) to ensure it is true, specific and timely. Then you enrich the information in one of the ways outlined. You proceed by ensuring that you are sending quality information to create as much value as possible.

We are looking to use external information in a way that is useful for our purposes. It must be based on quality information and enriched with another aspect, as illustrated below.

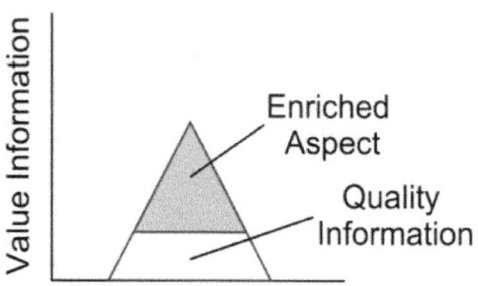

The raw information (B) that you have at this point does not fulfil all the requirements to be both relevant and accurate. In the following sphere, this will be addressed.

2nd Requirement - Factually True

Quality information needs to be based on sources. Even the most biased incoming information, is based on something. For quality information, that source must be factually true. In reality, there is oftentimes no way of knowing what the information is based upon.

Thus, the possibility of acquiring false knowledge clearly exists. In other words, this information is not based on something true. Instead, it was created to fulfill a purpose. Furthermore, it could also very well be that the information was deliberately stretched to qualify as both timely and specific.

False information in your thinking will make your decision severely less thoughtful and can even be more dangerous than ignorance. The use of false information in decision-making eliminates reasonable doubt and creates false certainty.

While it is possible to trace the material parts of the information back to their sources, there will always be a risk of false knowledge in your thinking. This dramatically impacts the ideal approach of receiving and transferring information with regards to this requirement.

Ideal approach in Receiving

It is reasonable to segment the incoming information in material and immaterial parts. Then, attempt to trace back material parts to either a trusted person or a trusted source of information.

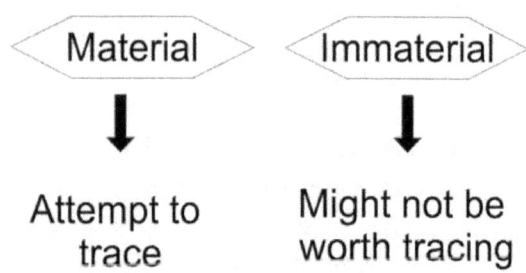

Nonetheless, the risk of false knowledge remains. Thus, you need to be more cautious and humble in what you think you know and what you intend to pass on.

Ideal approach in Transferring

Apart from exercising caution and humility, it is crucial that concerns regarding uncertain origins of information are disclosed upon knowledge transfer. You do not want to become a trusted person with potentially untrue information.

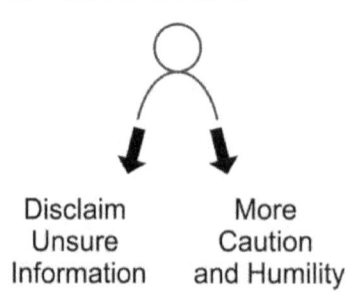

The Result

Recognizing the challenges and understanding the ideal approaches of receiving and transferring information, with regards to being factually true, is an important step towards quality information.

By covering the 2nd requirement on the way to quality information, you have ensured that it is accurate.

Now, you need to make sure it is relevant.

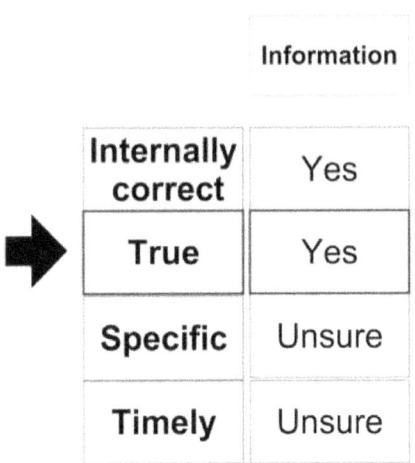

3rd Requirement - Specific

Information needs to be related to the issue in a way that is valuable. Specific information certainly depends on the purpose of the information. Nonetheless, it is always obtained by eliminating the clutter and the noise that does not directly support the information. The extent to which the clutter is eliminated is the differentiating factor.

Ideal Approach in Receiving

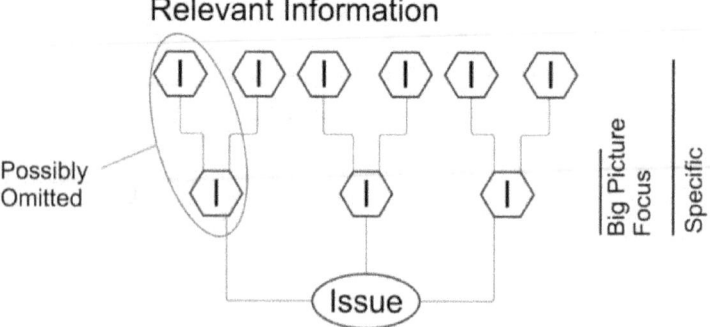

Naturally, specific information means that some of it has been omitted for the benefit of brevity. There might be information that has not been shared with you that could have been useful.

Unfortunately, you often have no way of knowing. Depending on the importance of the issue, you will need to gather more information or receive clarification. Always ensure that you have both specific and big-picture information to be able to base your thinking upon.

Ideal Approach in Transferring

The question that arises is: how much clutter do you remove in a consistent manner to obtain quality information with regards to specificity? Naturally, a trade-off occurs.

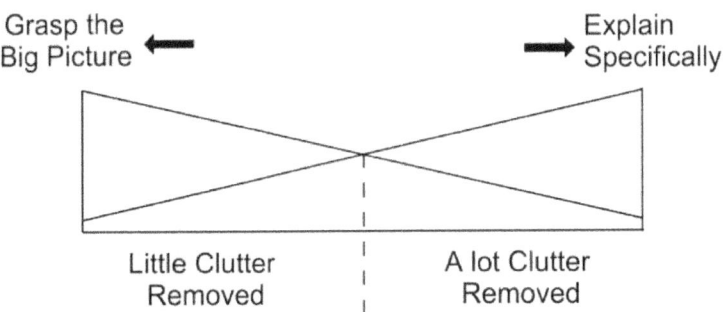

Too much specific information will make you lose sight of the big picture, but relate wonderfully to the issue. Too little specific information will allow you to see the big picture wonderfully, but relate less to the issue.

While this is contingent on the situation and the expectation of the subject onto whom you are transferring knowledge, you will attempt to be in the middle of this, already familiar, spectrum. Keep in mind, that depending on where you are on the spectrum, your secondary steps will be dramatically different.

If you are not being specific enough, you must focus (repeat transferred information) to relate to the issue more specifically. It requires initially more time, then less.

If you were too specific, you must explain (include new information previously not transferred) in order to grasp the big picture. It requires initially less time, then more.

The Result

By recognizing the challenges and understanding the ideal approaches of receiving and transferring information, and how each relates to specificity, you have made another important step towards quality information.

The 3rd requirement on the way to quality information has thus been covered.

	Information
Internally correct	Yes
True	Yes
Specific	Yes
Timely	Unsure

Now, you need to focus on the last requirement to obtain quality information.

4th Requirement - Timely

Ultimately, information always serves a future purpose. Thus, it needs to be received at a time that makes the information valuable.

It is crucial to realize that the usefulness of information with regards to time is dependent on the novelty of the information as well as its chances of remaining the same over time. This is illustrated below.

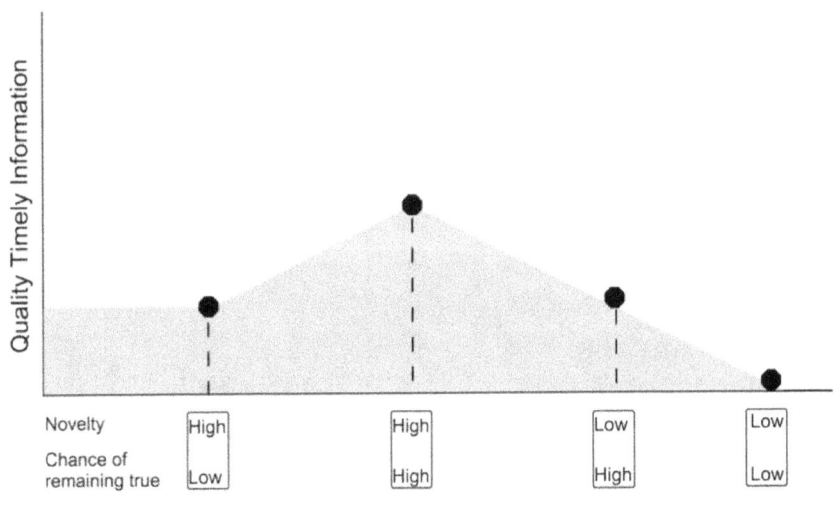

The novelty aspect of the information is less significant for information that tends to remain the same over time. In particular, information that does not change over time is deemed quality information with regards to time, irrespective of its novelty.

Ideal approach in Receiving

As illustrated in the previous graph, the most recent information might not always be the best information. It is just as important to understand if the information has a strong tendency to change. In order to adequately capture its quality with respect to time, ensure that you know both the novelty of the information as well as the chance of the content changing over time.

Ideal approach in Transferring

When transferring knowledge, pay attention to both its novelty and likelihood to change, and ensure that you disclose if one of those variables becomes negatively impacted.

The Result

Recognizing the challenges and understanding the ideal approaches of receiving and transferring information, with respect to timeliness, is the final step towards quality information.

	Information
Internally correct	Yes
True	Yes
Specific	Yes
Timely	Yes

By covering the 4th requirement, you have ensured that you have quality information.

The Enriched Aspect

You can add value to your environment in a multitude of different ways. As you share information, you will have a content benefit either way. Additionally, you may have a time benefit, an interpretation benefit or potentially both.

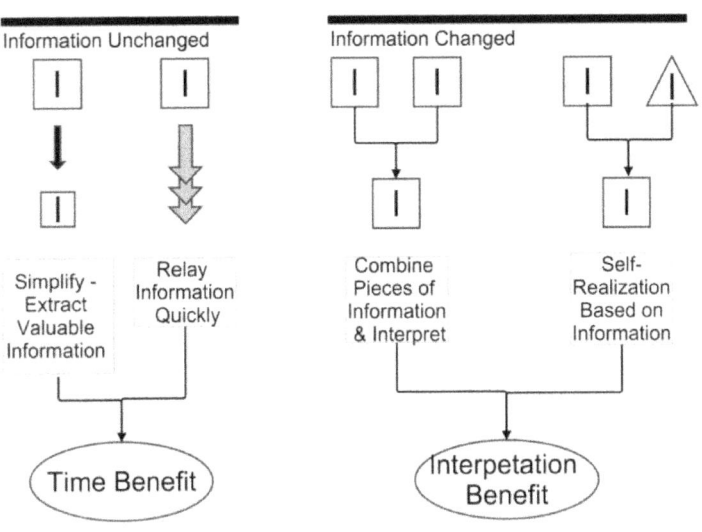

Time Benefit

There are two ways to add a time benefit to your content:

1. You can leave the information unchanged, and pass it on quickly, when needed. This approach is often practiced with non-complex pieces of information.

While this is a low risk and low effort activity, it still needs to be done in a thoughtful manner.

2. You can simplify and specify the information, thereby extracting valuable information. This will save the receiver of your information time, which naturally is a benefit.

It is vital to know that you can only simplify to a certain extent before you need to specify the information. Being specific means omitting information.

Interpretation Benefit
An interpretation benefit occurs when the transferred information exceeds the received information in value. Again, there are two options:

1. You can combine the received information with knowledge you already had to create new information that surpasses both individual pieces in usefulness.

2. You can interpret the information you have received without adding any new knowledge from another source. You evaluate the information with a goal in mind to attain self-realization.

Combining two pieces of information or attainting self-realization requires critical thinking, good judgment as well as previous knowledge. In both cases, you create new knowledge.

Summary

As you share information, you will have a content benefit either way, regardless of other benefits added. In other words, the information that you intend to pass on can take on one of three forms.

Information Benefit

Time	Interpretation	Interpretation
Content	Content	Time
		Content

→ Complexity

Naturally, adding different benefits influences the degree of complexity of the information.

Excursion - The Interpretation Benefit

The interpretation benefit within information is everywhere. Nevertheless, we are unconscious of its potentially enormous impact.

Every single great idea is the result of combining two or more smaller ideas, along with self-realizations that stem from expertise and creativity.

So, knowledge oftentimes brings along with it more valuable knowledge. In a very real way, it is self-creating.

Now, the art of combining ideas is complicated and way beyond my knowledge and the scope of this book. Nonetheless, I still made an effort in the coming pages to discuss the compatibility of different ideas, which may guide your thinking in this sphere.

Compatibility of ideas

Restrictions
The majority of ideas have individual restrictions, meaning instances where they cannot be applied. There is a tendency of putting less emphasis on these individual restrictions. In complex ideas, consisting of many individual ideas, one overseen restriction can cause a greater thought to become practically worthless.

Complexity
Combining two ideas naturally adds an extra level of complexity to the endeavour. There is a tendency to shy away from the newly arisen complexity, and prematurely dismiss ideas that complicate. However, these ideas are exactly the important ones, instead of avoiding this added complexity one should embrace colliding ideas.

Scope
When combining two or more ideas, the scope is decisive. There must be a balance between focusing on one aspect, and focusing on the big picture. Excessively operating in either pole will make combining ideas significantly more challenging, as you will either have too much information or not enough.

Independence
As previously mentioned, an interpretation benefit is dependent on the quality information that supports it. In other words, base your thinking on relevant and accurate information. Further, try to think from a place of an independent third party. If you are not involved in the issue or not knowledgeable of the issue, take yourself and your ideas fully out of the equation.

Openness
A valuable interpretation benefit takes time. Keep your mind as open as possible. Prematurely settling on ideas or conclusions, without explicit time pressure is counterproductive and will severely impact the quality of your thoughts.

Sphere C

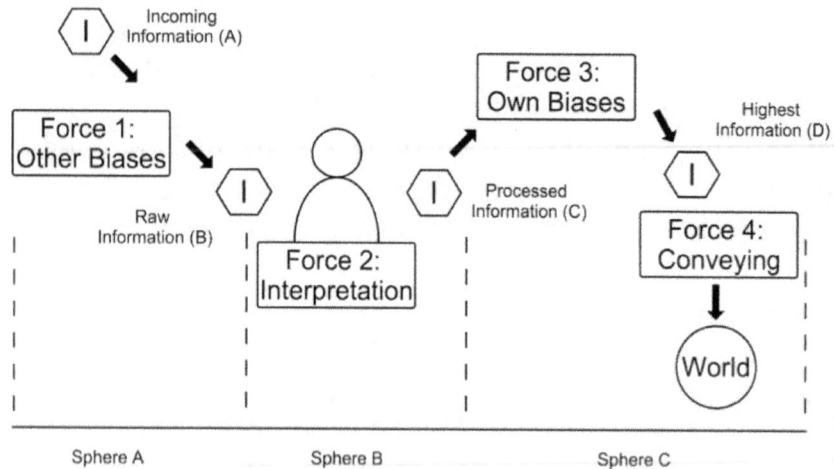

Guiding goal

You clean the processed information (C) of your own biases, thereby addressing the last requirement of being internally correct, and convey the information (D).

Force 3: Own Biases
The impact that biases have on one's self, when compared to others, is often underestimated. Both the internal and external biases will have impacted the processed information that you intend to pass onto your environment.
Thinking clearly means taking this into consideration.

By critically reflecting on the five major biases, you will be able to at least minimize their effect on your thinking, while also attaining more clarity.

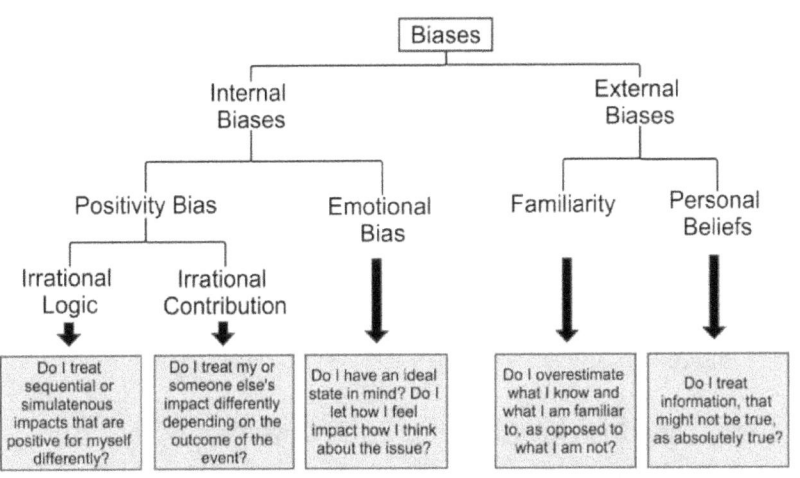

Recognizing the flaws in your own thinking is a great initial step. However, the biases need to be understood and potentially disclosed and/or actively mitigated with the approaches previously outlined.

Force 4: Conveying

At this point in the thinking process, you have the highest form of information (D).

Our knowledge at this particular point;
is both accurate and relevant,
is enriched with time benefit, content benefit or both,
and is free of your own biases.

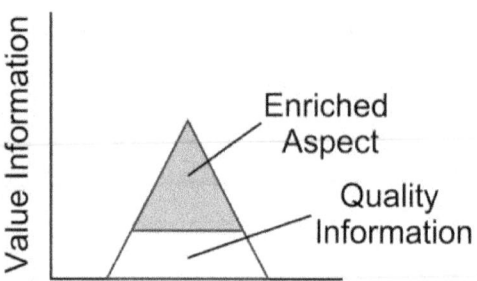

The last remaining step is to contribute as much as possible to the world by conveying information effectively in order to minimize information loss.

Information loss is the difference between what you know and want to contribute, and what the other subject knows after you conveyed your information.

On one hand, conveying information in written form will allow you to more easily minimize information loss, it is, however, far more time-consuming. On the other hand, conveying information verbally will risk greater information loss but minimize time required.

Conveying information in either medium has its merit. When you have the option to choose, it is largely dependent on personal preferences and the circumstances.

Conveying information in written form

Apart from writing legibly and clearly, your sentence should strive to convey information as simply as possible, without compromising content. You are either describing an event, explaining an issue, persuading someone, formulating an opinion or exploring an issue - choose your writing structure accordingly.

Conveying information verbally

Maintain eye contact to ensure that the person pays attention to you. Doing so adds credibility to your message, and exudes confidence. Leverage an adequate amount of physical gestures to guide the attention of the person to ensure that the key pieces of information are understood. Select an appropriate tone of voice depending on the situation to minimize information loss. Ensure alignment between what you say, content-wise, and how you convey it verbally. Keep a positive attitude towards yourself and the other person, and be present with your mind and your body.

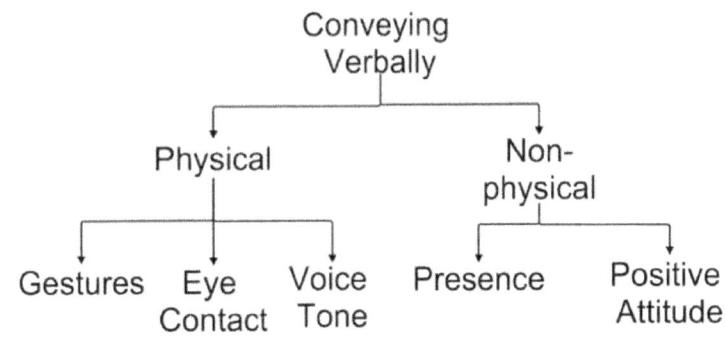

Excursion - Control within the framework

While all of these four forces are within your control, you will not be able to influence how your conveyed information is interpreted.

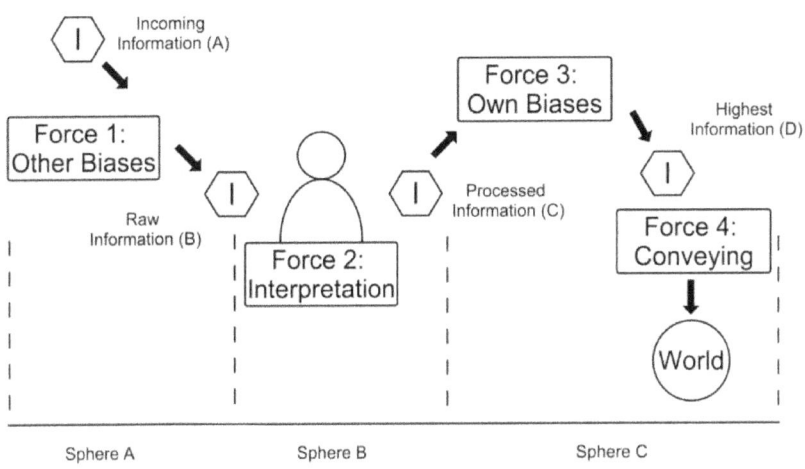

Once the information is sent, the interpretation of it is outside of your control. Thus, it is vital that you adjust the information, while it is still in your control, before transferring it to the environment. Meaning, stress certain aspects of your information to give the person the right impulses that will favour your desired interpretation.

Specifically, the knowledge that you are intending to transmit, has a targeted interpretation in mind. It will draw the subject to the one desired interpretation.

Closing Thoughts

This chapter introduced a roadmap that guides your thinking, along with fundamental concepts that are universally true and applicable. More specifically, it is about transmitting the right information.

The processes in these individual spheres often happen subconsciously. Nonetheless, drawing attention to the existence of these core concepts and providing a structure to one's thought process will inevitably make you think and understand more clearly.

Chapter 5:
Problems & Outcomes

Intro

Essentially, problems are just situations that are not ideal. We rarely find ourselves in ideal situations. So, there are really only problems around us - thousands of them. We have, and we will always face challenges, until the day we leave this world.

While this may be intimidating, I sincerely hope that you have the strength to face these challenges head on, and the humility and courage to reach out for help when it is needed.

In this chapter, I outline a series of core concepts around problem confrontation and problem solving, which should always be true and applicable to everything and everybody.

The Meaning of Problems

Our lives are a series of problems and solutions. Everyday, we encounter thousands of inconsistencies between what the world is and what we want it to be.

People often do not realize that they are solving most of our everyday problems subconsciously. Small problems often get corrected or solved in a few seconds without a moment's thought.

In other words, you have already solved the majority of your problems; you simply need to consciously solve the remaining few.

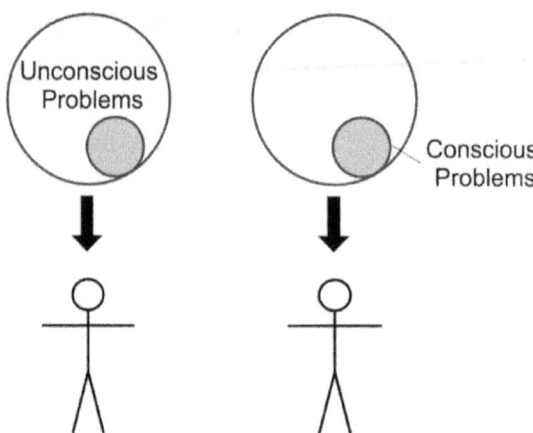

Life would be dull if all our problems were solved subconsciously. You would never be able to know who you are and who you could be. Furthermore, you would not be able to understand your limitations. At the end of the day, problems give us an identity in terms of how we identify, respond and grow as a result of them.

Fortunately for us, the world has given us problems that cannot be solved unconsciously - it has simultaneously given us an identity.

Your Problems

It is critical to understand what 'your problems' are.

In part, it depends on an important distinction between the various problems you will encounter. The same distinction will dictate whether you have to solve them or not.

You may encounter problems that will automatically require you to think. They cannot be ignored and require immediate or future solving. These are 'type 1 problems', which you must address.

You may also encounter 'type 2 problems'. They are disguised around you. As these problems do not require our attention or solving, they can be ignored and often are. In other words, they do not have to be addressed.

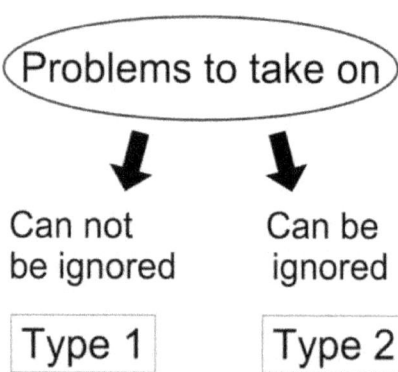

Thus, 'your problems' consist of all your 'type 1 problems' along with some selected 'type 2 problems'.

The question is: which 'type 2 problems' should become 'type 1 problems'? For which problems, that could have been ignored, will I invest time and effort to achieve a result?

To assess the significance of 'type 2 problems', I have depicted their respective worthiness to be accepted as a function of time-pressure, severity of the problem and effort required. This is illustrated below.

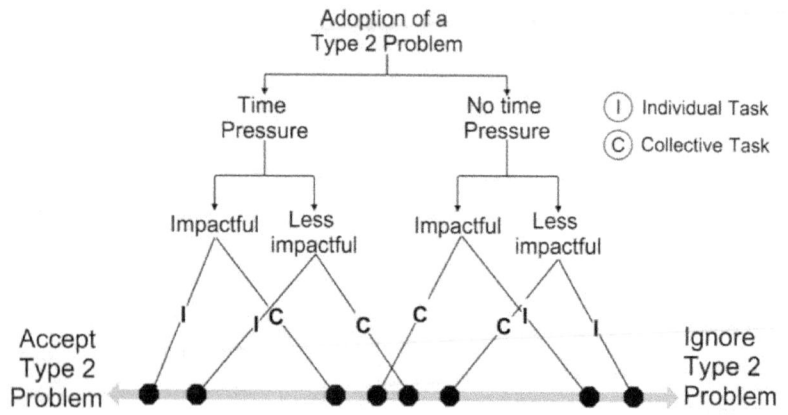

Time pressure
Intense time pressure deems immediate solving and attention necessary. Limited time simultaneously means that there might not be anyone better suited than you to solve the problem. This is especially true when the problem only requires individual effort. Fact is, the higher the time pressure, the more likely you should accept the 'type 2 problem'.

Impact of the problem
Every problem creates positive and negative feedback to a certain extent. The severity of a problem is determined by how much the negative feedback outweighs the positive. Naturally, the more severe a 'type 2 problem', the more likely you should accept it.

Effort required
As previously illustrated, I have categorized problems by the amount of effort they require to be solved. There could be one-person jobs (I) or jobs that require collective effort (C).

The decision to take on a one-person 'type 2 problem' is closely linked to time-pressure. Generally, the most suitable person willing to solve the problem should take it on. When there is time-pressure, this most ideally suited person tends to be you. The more time you have, the more likely it is that a person better suited to solve the problem can be found. Strictly speaking, the more time you have, the more likely you should ignore the problem.

For reasons beyond the scope of this book, deciding to address 'type 2 problems' that require collective effort, leaves a lot more room for ambiguity. These decisions are often motivated by the out-of-situation parameters.

Out-of-situation parameters

These parameters include, but are not limited to:

Moral obligations
Personal preference
Possibility of detachment
Personal or relatable impact
Assessment of the cause's need for own contribution
Social motivations

After deciding what 'type 2 problems' to take on, you will be able to understand what 'your problems' really entail.

Namely, all the 'type 1 problems' and some selected 'type 2 problems'. Remember that unlike 'type 1 problems', you will always have the possibility to not address 'type 2 problems'.

Priority of Problems

Now that you understand what 'your problems' are, it becomes a matter of assessing their priority. It is critical to understand that priority is primarily evaluated "based on time", and secondly "based on impact".

Primary Criteria - Time

Time is the most influential factor in prioritizing problems. Naturally, every problem has either a deadline, suggestive or absolute, or an open-end.

In the case of problems with deadlines, the due date is decisive in their prioritization, as they naturally need to be resolved by that point.

Furthermore, as illustrated, problems with deadlines outside of your control will have a higher priority.

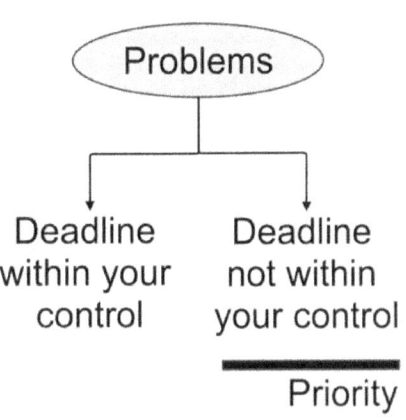

If the deadlines are within your control, you may have the opportunity to push back the deadline. This allows for more time to resolve the problem, but also risks a change in the problem's magnitude for future solving.

You will have to decide if the action of pushing back the deadline, along with all accompanying side-effects, is worth it. Specifically, considering the extra time and resources that you will have at your disposal by not solving that problem at that time.

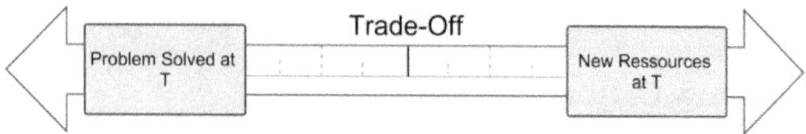

Some problems are open-ended, meaning, there is no pre-determined time for which they must be resolved. Nonetheless, time still influences the priority of those problems as their magnitude could change.

As long as the problem is solving itself, you should let it, unless the time to solve it becomes unacceptable.

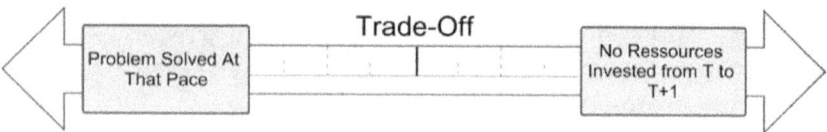

If the problem is increasing in magnitude, you will have to weigh the benefit of not investing time and effort at point T versus the benefit of the problem being solved at point T.

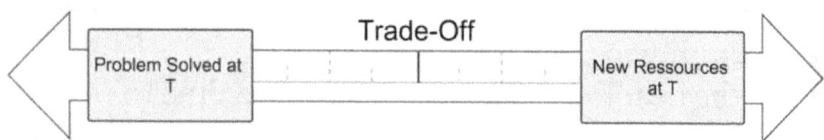

Secondary Criteria - Resource and Impact Relationship

Time, as well as its accompanying trade-offs, is the primary factor in prioritizing problems.

The solving of any problem will require resources and will have an impact. The term 'resources' includes both time spent and effort made. The relationship between resources invested and the value of the impact is the secondary factor deducing the priority.

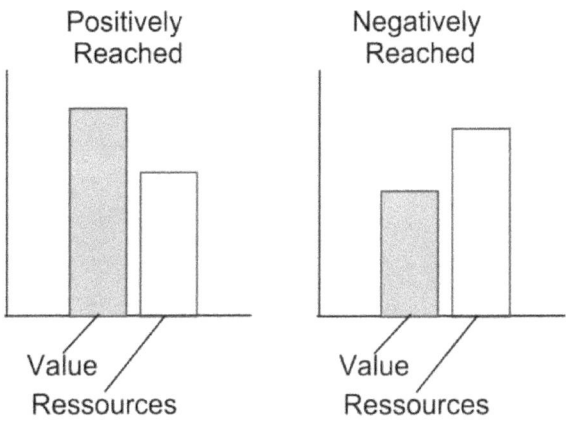

Keep in mind that resources used and impact achieved are in relation to each other. The ratio of how much impact you get for resources invested is critical.

Prioritizing your problems

In order to bring structure into the process of prioritization, it is useful to illustrate it graphically. This graphical representation of prioritization will enable us to identify our problems and assess their need to be solved.

As it can only contain problems up until a certain point in time, the graphical representation requires a time scope. A month's time is always a good place to start. The next step is to graphically indicate a point that corresponds with both the time requirement and the impact/resource ratio. In locating the problem point, you will have to ask yourself two questions.

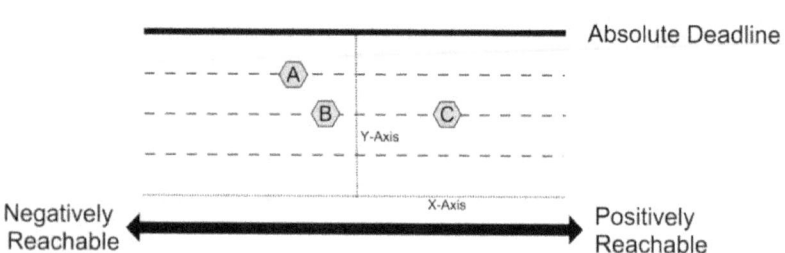

1. How much time do I have until the problem must be solved? This will tell you the value of the y-axis. The more time that is available to solve the problem, the lower the value of the y-coordinate.

2. How beneficial is the rate between the impact achieved and the resources invested? This will tell you the value of the x-axis. The higher the ratio is, the higher the value of the x-coordinate.

As previously illustrated, 'problem A' will still have a higher priority than 'problem B', regardless of its position on the x-axis. Additionally, 'problem C' has a higher priority than 'problem B', as it is more beneficial and has the same time pressure.

Confronting Problems

Now, it is your responsibility to solve all your 'type 1 problems' and, if possible, some 'type 2 problems'. In this section, we will focus exclusively on problems that require your personal effort. Before confronting your problems, there are three factors to consider that are absolutely vital. You must be willing to solve the problem and it must be possible to solve.

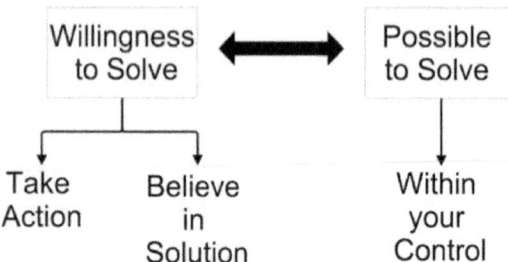

As depicted above, you will need to be willing to take action, willing to believe in your solution and the problem must be within your control.

Willingness to take action
You intend to actively address the issue, investing both time and effort.

Believing in one's own solving approach
You must believe that what you intend to do will solve the problem or has a good chance to do so.

Within your control
It must be possible for you to approach the problem in some way.

The factors illustrated below must be present in order to successfully confront a problem. To demonstrate the reason for this, imagine confronting a problem while deliberately neglecting one of these aspects. Interestingly enough, there are valuable insights to be learned in these three scenarios.

The solving of a problem is within your control and you believe in a possible solution, but you choose not to take action.
Simply desiring a change, will not result in a problem's resolution.

The solving of a problem is within your control and you are willing to take action, but you do not believe in the solving approach that you possess.
Not every solving approach will resolve the problem.

You are willing to take action, and you believe in your solution, but the problem is outside of your control and influence.

Things that are beyond one's control are not relevant.

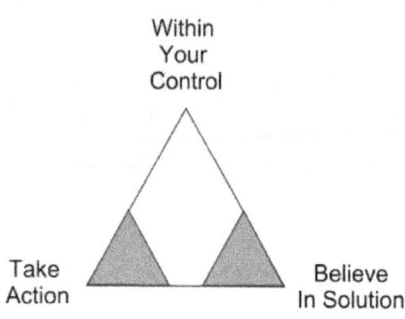

Impact of the Path Not Taken

In choosing a path to move forward, you are simultaneously deciding to not undertake all other paths. We have previously touched on the matter of paths not taken. As seen below, the number of paths not taken is overwhelming.

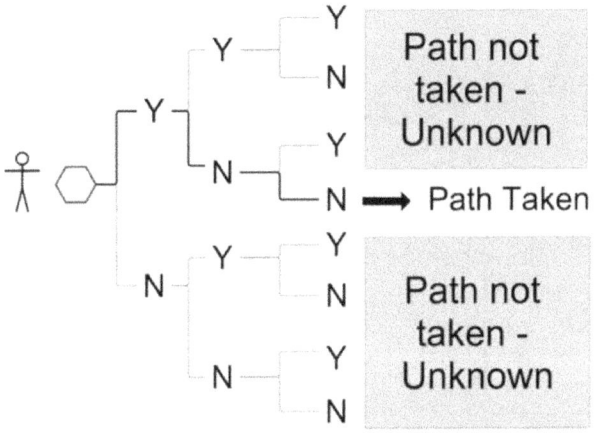

There is a tendency for one to focus on how people have solved problems. It is far more important, and difficult, to focus on how the problem was not solved.

The focus is usually placed on what we know happened, and not what could have happened if another path was chosen. Obviously there is a great deal of uncertainty regarding the outcome of another potential solving approach, as it was never actually undertaken.

Undoubtedly other people will judge the quality of your solving approach and the result that was achieved.

Interestingly enough, they can only base their opinions on what could have happened in a different scenario, irrespective of the nature of the actual outcome. In essence, they will judge your decision based on what could have been.

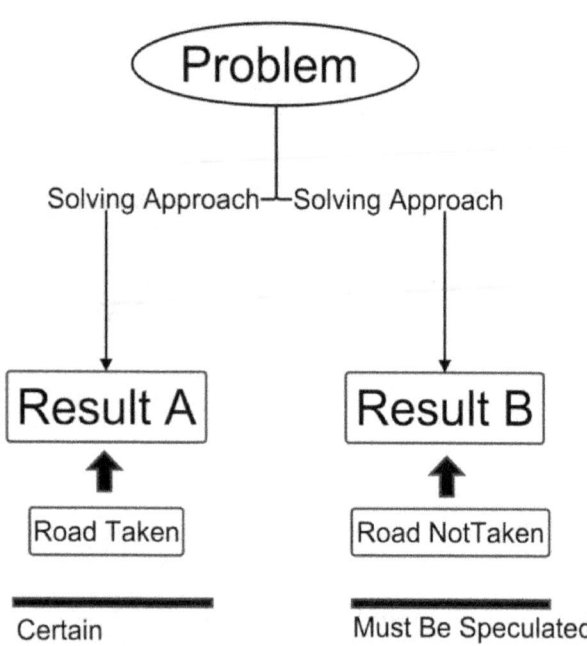

This aspect has a significant impact regarding the perception of your decision. Regardless of the nature of the potential outcome, the uncertainty will always diminish the validity of criticism and praise.

In other words, the praise as well as the criticism of your decision will be diminished. This is illustrated below.

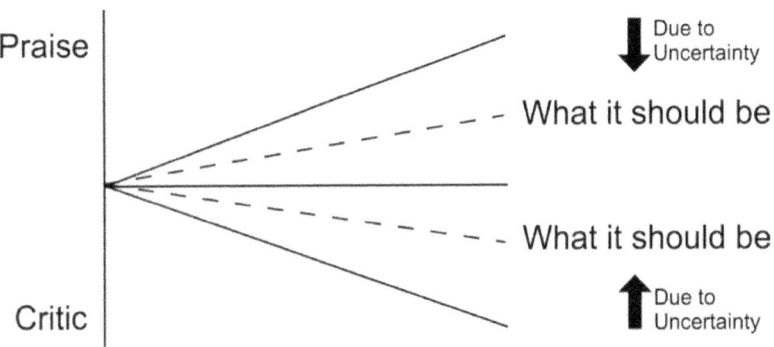

Since no one can know with certainty what could have happened, if you would have taken a different path, your decision will and should be both less praised and less criticized.

The benefit of receiving less extreme feedback about your undertaken solving approach is worth recognizing for any decision-maker.

Closing Thoughts

Permanently solving problems is our reality. You are doing so, constantly, whether you realize it or not.

The purpose of this chapter was to bring clarity to your understanding of 'your problems', to address prioritization, and to introduce the impact of the path not taken.

As these insights are always true and applicable to everything and everybody, they may even guide your thinking to a certain degree.

Chapter 6:
The Essential Eight

Intro

The purpose of this book was to outline valuable core concepts that are both always true and applicable to everything and everybody. As such, a series of relevant special topics were included.

Naturally, I was not able to include all the topics that will undoubtedly stay relevant over the next thirty years. However, eight fundamentally essential life lessons were included.

Self-Control

Exercising self-control means regulating your own desires.

Self-Control is the prerequisite of a thoughtful life, as most things that will contribute to such a life will not be intrinsically pleasant to do.

The ability to deliberately take the hard path, despite the presence of an easy path is called self-control.

The hard path often has a potential reward. In essence, it is the ability to delay gratification of going the easy path and, instead, go the more difficult path to obtain a reward in the future.

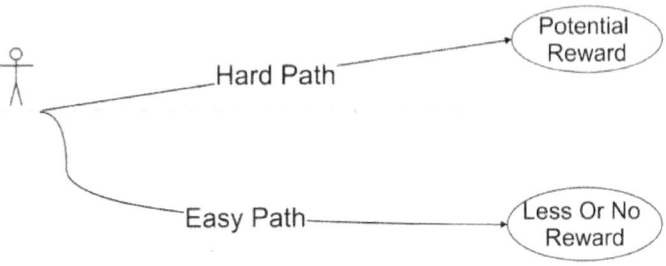

Even though the importance of delaying gratification might seem obvious, it is rarely ever practiced. Naturally, the reward or the outcome has to be worth the hard path. Fortunately, the things we really want will generally make the efforts worthwhile.

Nonetheless, the easy way is tempting, as it offers immediate gratification. There is a possibility to reward yourself prematurely. This is similar to taking a short-term instead of a long-term approach.

It is important that you comprehend what you are foregoing by not going the harder way. If you are fully aware and accept it, then this is your choice. However, it is important that this choice was made thoughtfully.

I sincerely hope that you have the wisdom to distinguish the easy way from the hard way and the self-control to rationally choose which of the paths you want to go.

Self-Control in addressing problems

Solving problems is in itself, a reward. Nonetheless, it entails a crucial difference. All of your problems must be addressed in some way or another. This simple aspect is so critical.

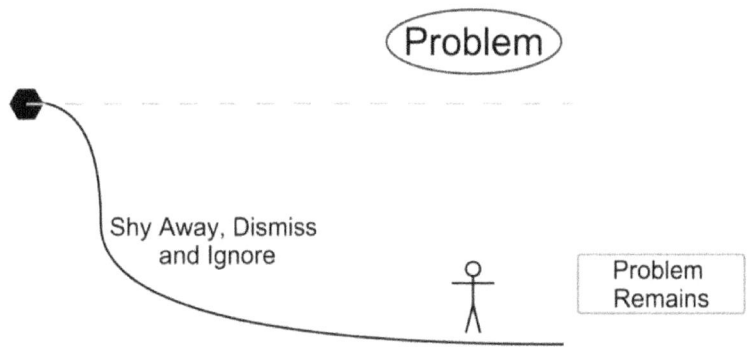

The easy way

You can easily follow your natural instinct and shy away from the negative. Thereby, you ignore or dismiss the problem. It is easy. Unfortunately, the problem remains.

In essence, you encountered a problem that was not going to solve itself and your conscious decision was to do nothing.

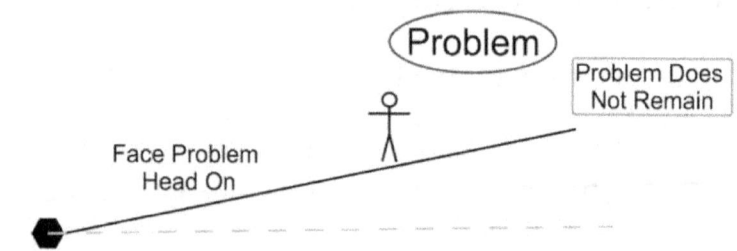

The hard way

You can also consciously reject your natural instincts and be drawn to the negative.

Remember that the reward of your effort is a solved problem, along with the fact that you will not have to deal with it again. Confronting problems head on, while having the choice to ignore them, is highly admirable.

In essence, you encountered a problem that was not going to solve itself and you did something about it.

I wish you the wisdom to identify the problems that will not solve themselves, as well as the strength and self-control to choose to confront them head on and without delay, all the while knowing you did not have to.

We all have our problems. While confronting them is our task and ours alone, we should have the humility and judgment to ask for help and advice if you cannot solve them. Your problems do not have to remain your problems alone.

Humility

Humility means having a modest estimate of one's own importance, along with a modest opinion. It means being conscious enough to recognize and accept your own limitations.

These limitations mean that you will never be able to be completely sure of yourself. Human error, along with the presence of uncertainty, will result in the fact that we know little for sure.

While you should not let your limitations control you, it does not mean, you should not respect them. Respecting them means humility.

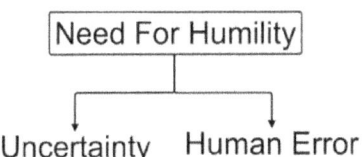

Being certain and humble are not mutually exclusive. There is no need to discard what you think you know, just because it might not be true. The point is that there is great virtue in being humble and open to realize that what you know will never be complete or accurate.

Respecting your limitations also means recognizing that others know more than you. Every person will be able to do something better than you, or knows something that you do not know.

If you want to grow as a person, you will need the self-control to recognize your limitations, the openness to see the strengths of others, and the willingness to learn.

Tolerance

Tolerance is the idea to live and think and let others live and think as well.

In other words, it is the quality of accepting ways of thinking that conflict with your own. It is the realization that your way is not the only way.

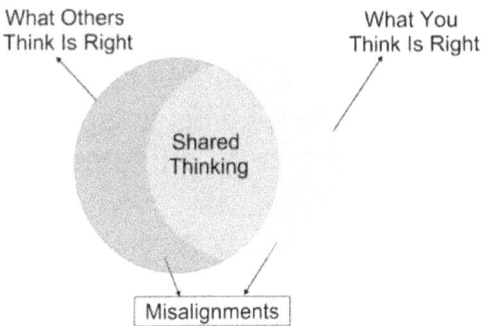

Not everybody thinks alike or acts alike. Throughout your life, what you think is right will never align exactly with what others think is right. These misalignments are natural.

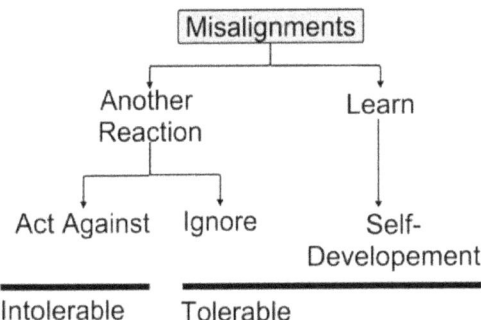

As seen above, the misalignments could spark learning and progress or it could lead to another reaction.

Learning and progress

These misalignments can serve as a learning opportunity. You may be able to adopt some of the beliefs, at your own discretion of course.

After all, what you believe to be right is largely dependent on the information you have received during your upbringing. In other words, it originated from people that had different views about what is right. Having the openness and the humility to see differences in thinking and living, as 'something that might be right' and not merely 'differences', is valuable.

Another reaction

It is possible that the difference between how you live and think and how others live and think misaligns in a way that may deem another reaction necessary.

You can ignore the misalignment, and let other people live just like they let you live. Or, you can act against it in some shape or form and be intolerant.

If you decide to be intolerant, please exercise the utmost caution. While it is a moral duty to not tolerate everything, correcting others is a highly complicated endeavour.

Keep in mind that in assessing tolerance you are trading off the benefit of addressing the misalignment against the virtue of letting people live. Ensure that you are guided by principles of fairness and justice, as well as common sense.

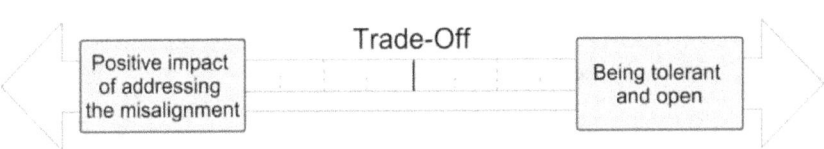

In conclusion, you should be able to accept ways of thinking that conflict with your own, be willing to see other perspectives and be open to self-doubt and learning. However, it is paramount that you do not permit the occurrence of intolerable acts for the sake of allowing people to live.

Feedback

Feedback is a necessary part of life. We constantly give and receive feedback, regardless of whether we want to or not.

Ideally, your actions should be thoughtful before they even allow for feedback from the environment within which you operate. Thus, praise should not motivate you any more than criticism should hold you back. Essentially, doing things solely for the reason of receiving positive feedback, or to avoid negative feedback, is in itself senseless.

If you let the perception and feedback of others dictate your behaviour entirely, you will never be able to grow as a person.

The point is for one to be dedicated enough, such that praise or criticism will not affect what one does, while simultaneously, being open enough to recognize when feedback has merit and embrace its guidance.

Receiving feedback

In essence, there are always three types of feedback you can receive, as illustrated below. Namely, there is helpful criticism, harmful criticism and compliments.

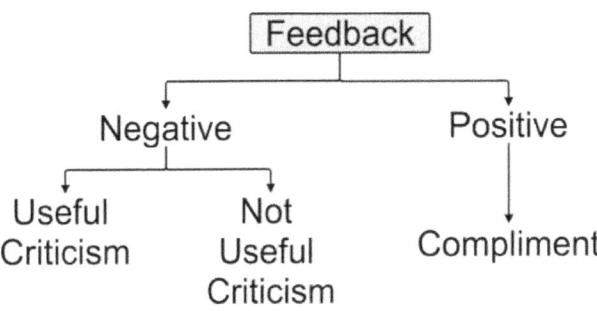

Compliments
Refrain from seeing positive feedback as a motivation, for it is not why you are doing it. Instead, look at positive feedback as a reinforcement of the positive nature of your actions, and a confirmation that you are probably on the right track. Nothing more. Learn to have the humility to thankfully accept compliments, but the strength not to be guided by them.

Harmful criticism
Throughout your life, you will be faced with negative feedback that one cannot learn from. It could be a short, vague, senseless and unclearly motivated act of feedback or even aggression. It is important that you have the confidence to dismiss this type of feedback immediately. Do not give it a second thought and continue on your path.

Useful criticism

Nearly all criticism has merit. Constructive feedback is rare, thus it must be endured and treated with no resentment. Be grateful for thoughtful feedback. Ignoring the possibility of your ways being flawed and in need of correction, is foolish. Dismissing this potential learning opportunity prematurely will prohibit you from growing as a person.

Letting Feedback affect you

In assessing the effect of feedback, think of three separate entities; feedback, knowledge and impact. As illustrated below, your first priority is to let positive compliments, as well as helpful criticism, transform into as much knowledge as possible.

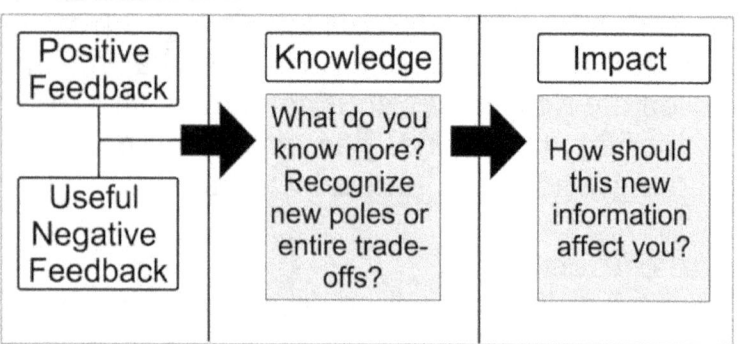

Then, after you have learned something new, you are able to reassess what you are doing. It is important that you do not decide or make conclusions right after the feedback is received. Instead, learn first, think for yourself and take your time.

Sending feedback

The actions of people around you are unquestionably worthy of your consideration. They deserve and simultaneously require that you think and offer constructive feedback.

Do not take this responsibility lightly. Your compliment or criticism must have an honest and true nature, and must be guided by good intentions. Attempt to invest enough thought, while providing the feedback as fast as possible.

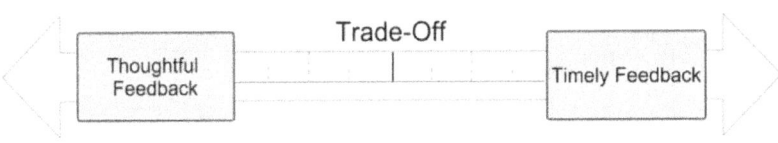

The presence of feedback is a blessing. Not because it motivates what you do, but because it can, and should guide you. There is great virtue in being open enough to allow the feedback to result in learning. This will empower you to improve your ways of thinking.

At the same time, you have a responsibility to provide the same benefit to people around you by offering timely and thoughtful feedback. It is only fair.

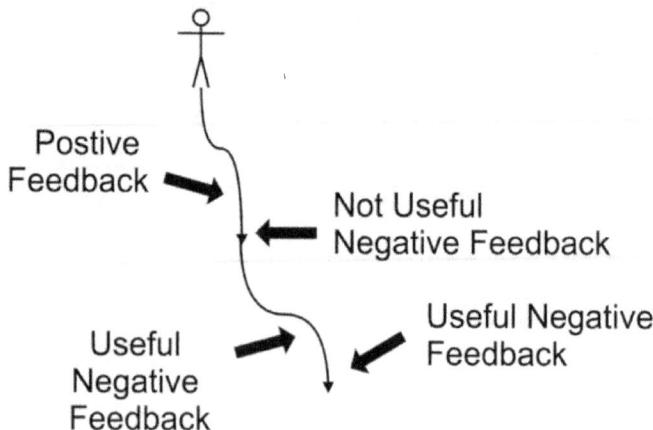

Time

Time is out of your control - it will go on whether you want it to or not. At the end of the day, it is all you have and you tend to overestimate how much you have left.

Time is precious enough to be managed. Understanding and managing time will make you more productive, and will enable you to lead a more thoughtful life. Managing time is guided by the principle that there should not be time for everything, but there must be time for the important things.

Managing time

Managing time is nothing more than addressing an issue at the right time for the right amount of time. Keep in mind that problems are simply situations that are not ideal. Leisure activities, similar to work activities, serve a purpose and thereby solve a problem.

When to address an issue

The proper time to address a problem will depend on its priority as discussed earlier in this book. Time is the first determinant of priority, followed by the ratio of impact achieved and resources needed.

As illustrated below, the nearer the problems are to the absolute deadline, the higher the priority.
Essentially, in deciding when to do something, focus on the time it must absolutely be done by, considering possible extensions of the deadline. The bold line can be seen as the ultimate deadline.

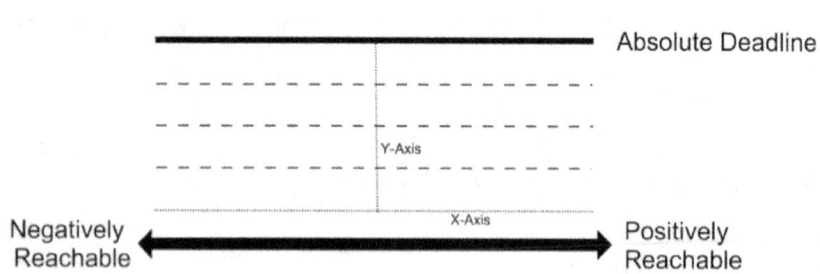

If two problems have to be solved by the same time, the problem that has a better impact-to-resource ratio will have priority.

How long to address an issue

Addressing an issue makes sense until the benefit of making an effort and spending time elsewhere exceeds the benefit of resolving the current problem. While that may sound obvious, it is hardly ever practiced. You must always work on the problem with the highest priority. The only time when you will stop solving a problem is when something arises that exceeds the current problem in one of three ways.

This is outlined below.

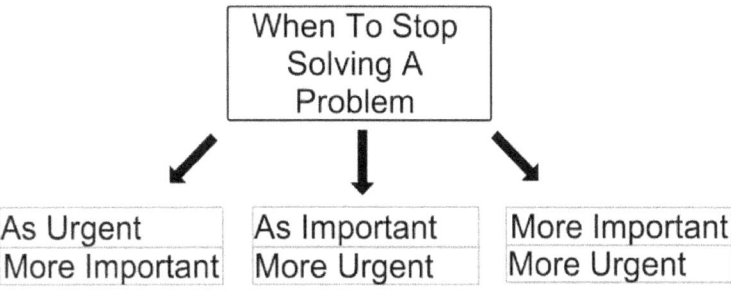

It is simply a reprioritization of what you have to do. Interestingly enough, this is also true for interruptions and distractions. Graphically, the area in which a task must be to require immediate attention is outlined below.

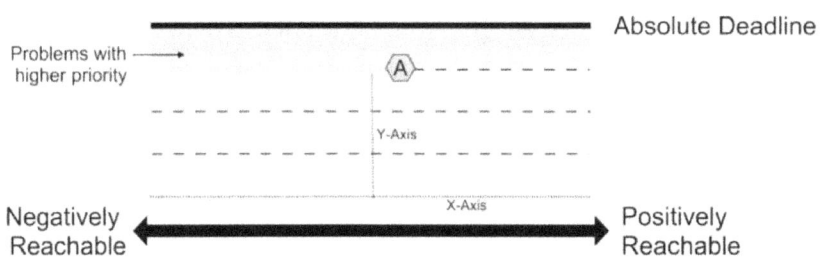

Self-Realization with regards to time

To avoid distractions, constantly push yourself to identify what problem you are currently solving and how much solving said problems is worth to you. When you are unsure about the benefit of what you are doing, you might want to reprioritize. Aim to push yourself to continually reflect upon the value of both leisure and work in relation to one another, and adapt accordingly.

Change

Change occurs when something has a different state.

Essentially, change happens when the status quo evolves into a new environment. Naturally, this occurs constantly. Throughout your day, you will have to decide numerous times how you will respond to change. The first critical aspect in assessing change, is determining if you can reverse it or not. In other words, is going back to the status quo an option? This is illustrated below.

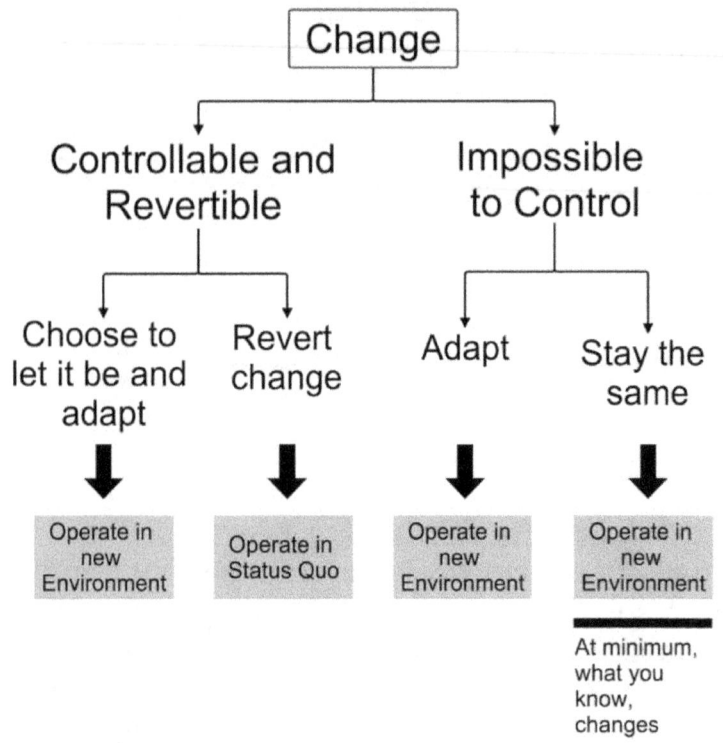

At minimum, what you know, changes

Reversible change

The key aspect of reversible change is that you have the choice between adapting to the new environment and going back to how things were.

If the new environment is not more advantageous for you, then you can simply go back. Nonetheless, going back often requires effort.
Thus, there is a trade-off.

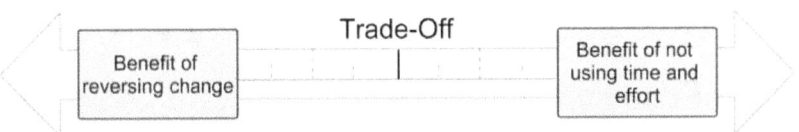

Irreversible change

The simple, yet misunderstood aspect of irreversible change, is that there is no status quo anymore - that environment has disappeared completely.

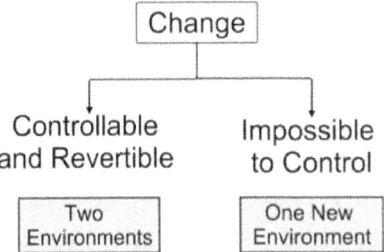

It is not relevant that the new environment might not be as advantageous. There is no going back to the status quo, regardless of time spent and effort made. Clearly, the choice is between adapting and staying the same. Even if you stay the same, your environment has changed, so what you know must change as well.

I will not be able to tell you what change is worth adapting for. Nonetheless, I can try to give you some guidance.

- Focus on the constants
- Focus on yourself
- Change your mind
- Potentially ➡ Change your actions

Step 1: Focus on the constants
Do not think of it as something that has changed. Think of it as "most things have stayed the same." Ideally, you would rethink your approach of not focusing on what is new, but focusing on what is still old and "the same." Then, and only then, focus on what has changed. You will not be able to know the essence of what changed, until you put it in relation to what has not.

Step 2: Focus on yourself
Almost automatically, you will think about how change impacts who you are, what you think and what you do. Remember that what you think you know is suddenly less valid than before. Try to see the new trade-offs that will surface based on the changed environment.

Step 3: Change your mind, and potentially change your actions
It is critical to understand that there must be an adaptation of what you know due to the irreversible change. While you do not necessarily have to adapt to the new environment, there must be a change of thinking. This change of thinking can potentially lead you to adapt.

Love

Love is all around us and it connects us with each other.

Giving love is a meaningful part of life that cannot be underestimated. Nonetheless, the degree of love given, in the form of positive energy or in another form or nature, will still need to be in balance.

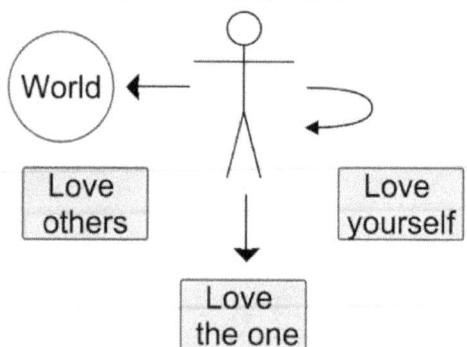

Love others

At the end of the day, everyone around us is struggling to some extent with personal problems. They all have a story to tell and unfortunately it is not always a happy one. People deserve nothing less than our kindness. The general rule must be to approach one another with compassion.

Even if kindness is not returned, it is no cause for disappointment. The goal will never be to have the whole world love you. Indeed, it is for you to love all the world.

Loving unconditionally can be just as wrong a path as not loving at all. The point is to be able to expand your understanding, to change your perspective, to adjust your thinking and to identify the positive, in order to spread love, while not giving it thoughtlessly and unquestioned.

Love yourself

You deserve your own love and appreciation just as much as other people do. The way to do that is through thoughtfulness and consciousness.

Earlier in this book, we discussed how our irrational thinking automatically and unconsciously overestimates the positive and underestimates the negative. In order to love yourself, you will need to do the exact same thing, but this time thoughtfully.

Try to deliberately empower the meaning of the good things in your life, which includes identifying new positive aspects. Simultaneously, attempt to reduce the meaning of the negative in your life, without decreasing the priority of problems that need to be solved.

It is paramount that you keep in mind that you are deliberately focusing on the positive. Doing this knowingly and thoughtfully will keep you in appropriate bounds.

Love the one

Trust that you will know when you need to know and that finding him or her is one of the greatest quests in your life - finding that one special person, however late, will make it all worth it.

Freedom

Freedom is having options moving forward.

We all have options. Therefore, we are all free to a certain degree, regardless of what is happening around us. In other words, you will always have at least two options. The only thing that will always limit your freedom is time - when your time runs out so does your freedom.

Essentially, you will have multiple paths ahead of you.

Freedom today is seen as being able to do whatever you want to do. That is not entirely accurate.

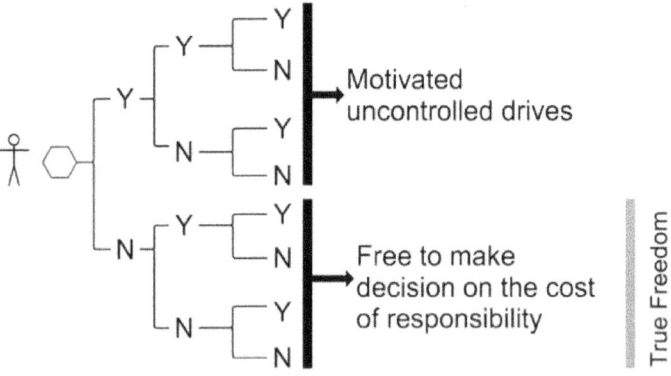

Undoubtedly, there are unconscious desires that, despite our efforts to control, translate into our actions. In other words, some of your actions are the result of urges that are not realized or understood. Blindly following them is not freedom, in fact, it might just be the very opposite. Thoughtfulness, situational awareness and self-control seem to be the only answer.

Obviously, you cannot do whatever you want. The consequences of your actions limit your freedom further. Whether you like it or not, you are always a part of the environment around you in some way. While you have a vast selection of different options, each path will inevitably lead to accountability - either to yourself or to your environment.

Thus, every decision comes with responsibility. Generally speaking, the more beneficial your path, the more responsibility you have to carry.

Essentially, there is a trade-off between responsibility avoided and benefits of a path.

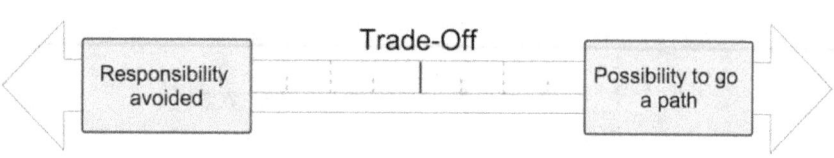

As illustrated above, the benefits of your path will be diminished for you to have less responsibility. Fact is, people that are willing to accept more responsibility, will be the ones who are prepared to take the more valuable path.

Chapter 7: Guidance for a meaningful life

Personal Interpretation of the Meaning of Life

Lastly, I have decided to include my personal interpretation of what life is all about. Please keep in mind that this last chapter is neither always true, nor applicable to everything and everybody. In fact, it is highly subjective.

Nonetheless, I have decided to include these very intimate thoughts on life.

The meaning of life is to...

...happily (1) and thoughtfully work (2) towards something that you are proud of (3), in good companionship (4).

I will expand on the individual parts of this statement separately to offer a more coherent explanation of its meaning.

(3) ... happily and thoughtfully **work towards something that you are proud of**, in good companionship.

Working towards something that you are proud of is one of the fundamental prerequisites of living a meaningful life.

Joy without work is appreciation, which is needed and valuable, but does not compare to the feeling of happiness. Happiness requires work, it is not given - it is earned. Happiness is the result of our choices. If not, what would be the point?

Indeed, we must be reaching for something. You must have goals - something that you will look back on and smile. This can come in multiple forms. There should be a series of goals, both short-term and long-term, throughout your life. As long as you proudly pursue them the choice of goals is wise.

In other words, find something you will be proud of, and that is worth working for. It can be whatever you want it to be.

The most hopeful thing is that, it is not dependent on time or the size of the goal, but merely on perspective.

You can always start pursuing something you are proud of. It is never too late to live a meaningful life. You do not have to reach the goal in order to be proud of your efforts. It is not hard to live a meaningful life.

(1)... **happily** and thoughtfully work towards something that you are proud of, in good companionship.

Naturally, working towards something you can be proud of might not always be easy. In fact, it might just be the most challenging path. Nonetheless, you must attempt to find joy even on a journey full of problems.

The only way you will find happiness on this path is by recognizing the necessity of these problems (1), and by developing a joy of solving problems and overcoming obstacles (2).

1. Necessity of these problems
Recognize that there must be problems. Your goal is not easily attainable by everybody. It should not be. The problems you are facing are there to keep the others away - those who want it less than you. Thus, these problems are necessary and overcoming them is worth it as long as the goal is.

2. Joy of solving problems
Our life is essentially a series of problems, until the day we leave this world. You will never live without any problems whatsoever; the only thing that changes is their priority. This rather harsh truth is necessary to realize that you must embrace the problems you encounter. After solving the first problem, try to transition the successful moment into motivating you to keep going, to keep solving and to keep moving forward.

(2)... happily and **thoughtfully work** towards something that you are proud of, in good companionship.

Working and living thoughtfully means making good choices along the way, exercising self-control and being conscious of your limitations.

Situational Awareness
Living thoughtfully means accepting the past as unchangeable, realizing the unlimited options moving forward, and recognizing that there are only some beneficial options, of which one is the optimal path. In conclusion, it is how it is, many options exist and few paths arise.

Exercising Self-Control
Working in a thoughtful manner is deeply rooted in self-control. This includes balancing the future reward of the hard path with the reward of the easy path, while keeping a clear head. It also should give us the strength to be able to confront problems that require solving, head on.

Recognizing Limitations
There is much less certainty than previously assumed. Even with the most careful evaluations, you will never be able to grasp the uncertainty that surrounds all of us and that impacts all of our decisions. While you should not let your limitations control you, it does not mean you should not respect them. Respecting them means humility and caution.

(4)... happily and thoughtfully work towards something that you are proud of, **in good companionship.**

At the end of the day, everything you do, all the pride from pursuing and even reaching your accomplishments, will mean startlingly little if you cannot share them with anyone. Companionship, and ultimately love, is what connects it all.

The supportive companionship of family, friends and loved ones will make the hard path less so and the joyous things more so.

The deep intimacy and mutual love, that ease the hard path and intensify the pleasure of life, are the most momentous experiences in our life.

Companionship can also come from God. The world is too overwhelming, too astonishing, and too wonderful to be an accident.

While companionship in life consists of the people around you, there will be one person that stands out.

Someone to rectify everything,
someone to belong to,
and someone who makes it all worthwhile.

That might just be the single most beautiful thing there is.

Last Thoughts

This book is for my children. I am hoping that in thirty years from now, in times that are far more complicated than the current ones, you will be reading these pages with a smile.

I sincerely hope that with this book, I was able to offer simple and certain insights that will be relevant when you are my age. Remember that life and all its choices are yours and yours alone. I simply tried to provide you with some guidance for a thoughtful life.

I will leave you with this.

Ensure that the initial focus is on fundamentals, do not let complexity mislead you and find refuge in simplicity.

The End

Disclaimer

The goal of this book was to compile my realizations and my knowledge about a very specific topic without basing it on external sources. However, I realize that there is the possibility that similar concepts, in full or in part, could exist. I will not make a personal profit as a result of this book and I have no intention of infringing copyright laws.

Copyright © 2016 by Jan Friedli

All rights reserved.
No part of this book may be used or reproduced, stored or transmitted in any manner whatsoever without written permission from the publisher, except in the case of brief quotations embodied in critical articles and reviews. Inquiries should be addressed to:

Jan Friedli, Herrliberg

All photos Courtesy:
Jan Friedli

www.ingramcontent.com/pod-product-compliance
Lightning Source LLC
Chambersburg PA
CBHW060851170526
45158CB00001B/311